CABINS

CABINS

A Guide to Building
Your Own Nature Retreat

DAVID & JEANIE STILES

ILLUSTRATIONS BY DAVID STILES

FIREFLY BOOKS

A FIREFLY BOOK

Published by Firefly Books Ltd. 2001

Seventh Printing 2012

U.S. Cataloging-in-Publication Data
    (Library of Congress Standards)
Stiles, David.
    Cabins : a guide to building your own nature retreat
David and Jeanie Stiles. —1st ed.
[176] p. : ill. (some col.) ; cm.
Includes index.
Summary : Illustrated guide to designing and building a
wilderness cabin, cottage or camp.
ISBN 1-55209-564-9
ISBN 1-55209-373-5 (pbk.)
1. Cottages. 2. Seasonal houses—Design and
construction. 3. Recreation homes. I. Stiles, Jeanie. II. Title.
728.7   21   2001   CIP

Canadian Cataloguing in Publication Data

Stiles, David R.
    Cabins : a guide to building your own nature retreat

Includes index.
ISBN 1-55209-564-9 (bound)   ISBN 1-55209-373-5 (pbk.)

1. Vacation homes – Design and construction – Amateurs' manuals.
I. Stiles, Jeanie. II. Title.

TH4835.S74 2001   690'.872   C00-932614-6

Published in Canada in 2001 by
Firefly Books Ltd.
66 Leek Crescent
Richmond Hill, Ontario, Canada   L4B 1H1

Published in the United States in 2001 by
Firefly Books (U.S.) Inc.
P.O. Box 1338, Ellicott Station
Buffalo, New York, USA   14205

Design by Interrobang Graphic Design Inc.
Illustrated by David R. Stiles
Photography by David and Jeanie Stiles unless otherwise noted
Front cover photograph by Jennifer Waryas
Printed in China

*The publisher gratefully acknowledges the financial support for our publishing program
by the Government of Canada through the Canada Book Fund as administered by
the Department of Canadian Heritage.*

CONTENTS

DEDICATION

We dedicate this book to all those who dream of escaping to their own cabin, especially to Jean Trusty Daniel, a modern-day pioneer, starting life over in her Santa Fe "casita."

ACKNOWLEDGMENTS

We would like to thank the many friends and acquaintances who have shared their cabin experiences and lore with us, especially David Hense, Don Metz and Don Gesinger—all inspired cabin builders themselves. We would also like to thank Michael Worek and Lionel Koffler for their continued support and enthusiasm for our design ideas.

FOREWORD

In North American culture, the cabin holds a unique place in our collective consciousness. Enshrined in the best traditions of grass-rooted nostalgia, the cabin symbolizes those bedrock frontier virtues of self-reliance, sturdiness, simplicity, humility and—by inference—*honesty.* By its very lack of pretension, the cabin connotes a purity of life whose loss we yearn to recall. As a genre, it stands at the moral center of a particularly American ethos defined by a cast of characters as diverse as Abe Lincoln, Davy Crockett and Henry David Thoreau.

During the colonial era, the cabin was home on much of the frontier, and is still remembered in folklore, song and verse as a safe and cozy haven. Today, the notion of the cabin as Home Sweet Home persists in literature and film. Whether in the mountains, on the prairie or by the lake, it remains a symbol of all that we value.

Today, the cabin has become the place we get away to when the place we're in has worn us out, a retreat from anxiety, a place dedicated to renewal. From the moment we lift the latch, push open the door and inhale that smoky-creosote-camphor cabin scent, we are altered for the better. More than a home away from home, the cabin reminds us of how—we like to think—life used to be lived in simpler times. It provides us with an opportunity to be closer to nature, and closer still to one another. The cabin is where we go to replace the hum of technology with the buzzing of insects, where cyberspace is out of place, where a mouse still has two ears and four legs. The cabin is a simple, sacred place where food and drink always taste better, where music sounds brighter, where evenings with loved ones linger longer into pleasure, where sleep is deep and dawn is fresh with wonders we've elsewhere forgotten.

Cabins seeks to address not only the practical issues involved in the design and building of a cabin, but also to encourage the impulse. Life is long, but need it be so hectic?

Imagine: After a long drive into nightfall, you step out of your car onto familiar footing—not asphalt, not concrete—but the stuff of millennial forests and plains and shorelines, the earth itself. You stretch your tired body, and you know immediately that every traveled mile was worth it as long as the trip ended here. Within moments of your arrival, it seems as if a blanket of peacefulness has gently covered you. An owl calls from a distant treetop, the same hoot-hoot, hoot-hoooot you remember from the last time—*welcome back.* You breathe the night in deeply and look up at the stars. How could you forget they could be so dazzlingly bright? And the pines, the fragrance—the scent of sage or the salty air.

You drag your duffel bag up onto the porch and reach for the key hidden in the abandoned wren's nest above the door. The lock has its eccentricities, but even in the dark, you know how to coax it open; after all, you installed it yourself. When the groceries have been put away and the lamps are lit low, you light a fire. And as you sit back in that comfy, old chair and look into the lazily flickering flames, you can't begin to imagine what life would be like without the elemental pleasures of a cabin.

—Don Metz, architect

INTRODUCTION

When we told friends we were writing a book about cabins, invariably their response was, "What exactly do you mean by a 'cabin'?" *The Random House Dictionary* defines a cabin as "A small house or cottage usually of simple design and construction. . . for more or less temporary occupancy." However, we have found it to be much more than that. Everybody, it seems, has a different idea of what a cabin is. No longer is a cabin simply a small, often dark one-room structure as in the days of pioneers. In the Adirondacks, during the turn of the century, wealthy families like the Vanderbilts and Rockefellers built what they called log "camps." Although rustic in style, they were often enormous structures that held extended families and housed walk-in stone fireplaces. In southeast Canada, smaller structures, called "cottages," are often built on lake shores and used as weekend retreats, for fishing and swimming. In western Canada and many sections of the United States, the same structure is simply referred to as a "cabin."

This book has been written to help you fulfill your personal dream of cabin living. It includes everything you need to know about designing and building your own cabin. The book takes you through the entire process, from choosing the right land, to deciding how big and what style of cabin you want and how to outfit and furnish it. The cabin designs are illustrated with floor plans to give you some suggestions for dimensions and building techniques, but they can and should be adapted to fit your specific circumstances and needs.

Famous Cabins

The rich and the poor alike have built and lived in cabins at different times and for different reasons. Cabins have an important place in our history. The first settlers in North America built cabins to live in when they arrived on our shores. Later, the pioneers and frontiersmen who settled the west built similar homes. Writers throughout history have used cabins as retreats in which they could write in peace without distractions.

Robert Frost

Whose woods these are I think I know
His house is in the village though . . .

In 1921, Robert Frost moved to Vermont where he was a professor at Middlebury College until his death in 1963. During the summers, he lived in a cabin several miles from town, near what is now known as Bread Loaf Writers' Conference.

The cabin was built using log slab siding over asphalt felt and contained all the necessities that a writer needed. The cabin still sits on the same site today and is open to the public during the summer months.

Robert Frost's Writing Cabin

Abraham Lincoln

I was born, and have ever remained, in the most humble walks of life.

The cabin that is thought to be Lincoln's birthplace has been preserved and enclosed in a memorial building at the Abraham Lincoln Birthplace National Historic Site, in Hodgenville, Kentucky. Built out of native, hand-hewn hardwood, possibly by Lincoln's father, the cabin measures 16'x18' and was heated by a stone-lined fireplace with a chimney made of straw and hardwood. The three-quarter high chimney was not unusual in those days. It reportedly created less draft and therefore drew less heat up the chimney, allowing more heat—and smoke—to remain inside. There was a dirt floor and one window that was probably covered with greased paper or animal skin to keep out the winter cold. Lincoln, his sister and his parents lived in this tiny cabin for the first two years of his life and then moved on to a nearby farm on Knob Creek.

Abraham Lincoln's Cabin

Henry David Thoreau
In wildness is the preservation of the world.

In 1845, Thoreau built and moved into a one-room cabin on Walden Pond where he wrote his famous book, *Walden*. The original cabin was destroyed after Thoreau moved out, however, a replica was built using illustrations and dimensions from Thoreau's writings. The original site of the cabin consists of piles of rocks and rubble, the remnants of the original foundation. A reconstruction of Thoreau's cabin sits on the banks of Walden Pond in Concord, Massachusetts and is well worth visiting. A well-maintained path travels the circumference of the pond, making a pleasant half-hour walk, and the Thoreau Society Shop at Walden Pond is filled with useful information and insights into the life of Thoreau.

Thoreau built this cabin for $28.12. He cut all the timbers from local trees, carefully notching

Thoreau's Cabin

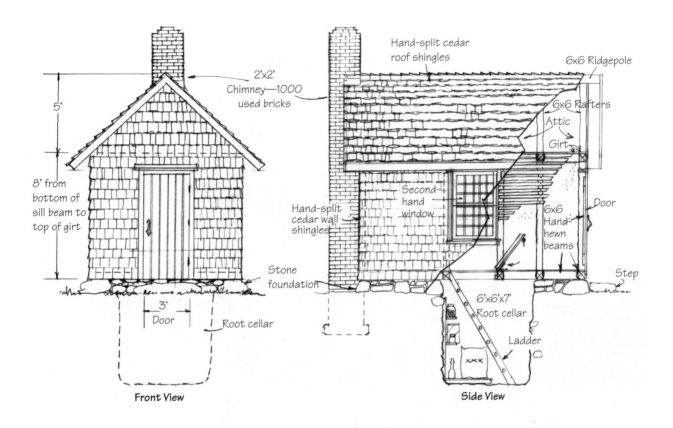

Front View

Side View

them "at the stump," and later planted 400 trees to compensate for the ones he cut down. He hand-split all the shingles that he used on the sides and roof of his cabin. Some of the material that Thoreau used was recycled lumber, bought from the local Irish workers, who had been living in shacks while building the railroad tracks near Walden Pond. Thoreau was also an accomplished mason, building the fireplace and chimney by himself, something that requires skill and know-how. The second year that he spent in the cabin, Thoreau installed a wood-burning stove in the fireplace. Although this made it easier for him to cook and heated his cabin more efficiently, he did mention that he missed watching the fire: "I felt

as though I had lost a companion. You can always see a face in the fire."

The inside of the cabin was plastered with a mixture of lime and horsehair. Underneath the floor was a 6'x6'x7' high root cellar, accessible by a trap door. It was here that he stored the vegetables he grew and harvested himself. Another trap door, in the ceiling, gave Thoreau access to a storage attic. A single bed, a round table with three legs, a writing table facing the lake and three chairs, named "Solitude," "Friendship" and "Society" (after the essays by Emerson with the same names), filled the interior of the one-room cabin. He wrote at night by oil lantern. Although he never locked his

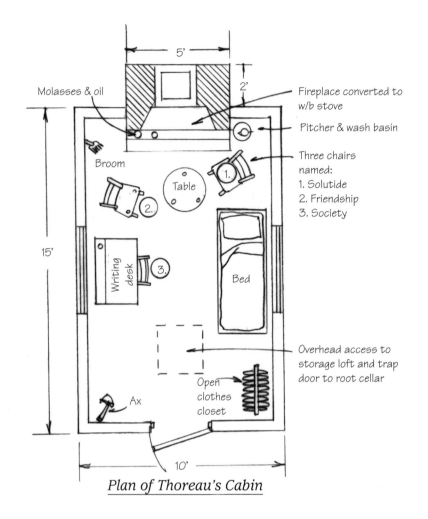

Molasses & oil

Fireplace converted to
w/b stove

Pitcher & wash basin

Broom

Three chairs
named:
1. Solutide
2. Friendship
3. Society

Table

15'

5'

2'

1.

2.

Writing
desk

3.

Bed

Open
clothes
closet

Overhead access to
storage loft and trap
door to root cellar

Ax

10'

Plan of Thoreau's Cabin

front door, his writing desk was kept locked when not in use.

A copy of Thoreau's original cabin can be built either by using timber framing, as Thoreau did, or by framing the walls with 2x4s or 2x6s. The floor joists should be 2x8 lumber and the rafters made from 2x6 lumber with a cross-tie every four feet. If you want to use the upper space for a storage loft, as Thoreau did, place cross-ties every two feet instead of every four feet and build a flat ceiling, using 1x10 rough sawn boards for the loft floor. Thoreau left a square opening in the ceiling to reach his storage space and presumably accessed it using the same ladder he used to climb down into his root cellar.

Thoreau covered the inside walls with plaster and horsehair; however, you may want to use insulation and sheetrock. You can give the walls a hand-plastered look by painting them flat white, mixing sand in with the paint. To remain true to Thoreau's philosophy, look for second-hand windows at salvage yards and antique shops and recycle them into your cabin.

With the increasing pace of modern life, the invention of cell phones, modems, faxes and beepers, the desire to escape and to return to a simpler life has an even greater importance. The cabin, a structure that in the past was a necessity, has now become a sanctuary, a place to escape from the rigors of everyday life and return to the land, even if only for a weekend.

CABIN PLANNING

Once, in fact, I built a house. It was a minuscule house, a one-room, one-floored affair set in the ivies and vincas of the backyard, and made almost entirely of salvaged materials. Still, it had a door. And four windows. And, miraculously, a peaked roof, so I could stand easily inside, and walk around. . . . It seemed a thing of great accomplishment, as indeed, for me, it was. It was the house that I had built. There would be no other.

—Mary Oliver, *Winter Hours*

To make your dream a reality, the first thing to determine is how far you are willing to drive before arriving at the cabin. If you are lucky enough to find undeveloped land between 30 and 60 miles of where you live, that is ideal. Start by taking a road map and draw a circle with a sixty mile radius around your home. Then consider the following points about any area that interests you:

- How congested are the roads leading to this area? Do they provide an enjoyable drive?

- Are there supplies available? Is there a convenient market, gas station, hardware store, lumber store? Are the land taxes high?

- Is there a lake, stream, river or ocean nearby?

- Do the people in the area seem friendly?

- Is property available at a reasonable price?

- Is there a hospital nearby?

- Will there be major development in the near future?

When you are looking for property, another useful map is a government survey topographical map that shows the lakes, streams and hills in the area.

As you drive around, ask questions. Talk to local residents, gas station attendants, store owners, anyone you run into. We found our land by chance, after asking someone, who was raking leaves, for directions. She just happened to know a neighbor selling a tract of land. Be optimistic—word of mouth is often the best way. Keep a log of information and make appointments directly with property owners, if possible. Brokers can be useful, but it is often easier, faster and less expensive to deal directly with a landowner. Buy the local newspaper and look for lots and acreage for sale. Take out an ad in the local paper and run it for a month. Enlarge and make copies of the same ad and put fliers up in local supermarkets and hardware stores, etc. Trace your route on the government survey map and note any available lots, recording pertinent information. Make sure

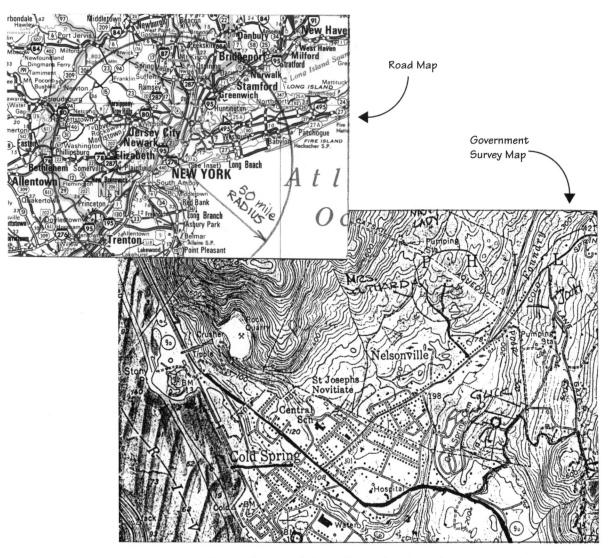

Road Map

Government
Survey Map

to bring along a clipboard, notebook and pencil, to take notes while you are exploring.

Larger circulation newspapers often list land for sale in the real estate classified section. Also check real estate magazines that cover your area. Once you've found an area you like, ask the local town clerk if any land is being auctioned off. Tremendous savings can be made this way, since these sales are seldom advertised and few people know about them. The Internet has also become a useful tool for searching for real estate.

Visit land you are interested in during different seasons. Photograph the land and record the location and time of year. Let yourself be known, locally. Look for signs, "For sale, by owner." Wear serious hiking boots and bring a camera. You may find a local farmer who needs to replace an old tractor, wants some fast cash and is willing to sell off some tree-filled land on the back forty, near a stream.

Once you find land that looks promising, some important considerations are:

1. Access. What kind of access is there to your building site? What kind of access do you require? Do you mind hiking and carrying supplies or do you need to have a cleared road?

2. Utilities. If you intend to have electricity and a telephone in the cabin, how far is it to the nearest utility pole?

3. Water. Is there fresh water nearby? How difficult was it for the closest neighbor to dig a well? Try to pick a spot near a pond, lake or existing well.

4. Contamination. Is there any evidence of soil contamination from an old dump? Is radon a problem in this area? Are there any neighboring farms that are spraying with chemicals that may have leached into the water supply? Is livestock contaminating a nearby stream?

5. Building site. Does the property have a buildable site, one with a view? Is it protected from the prevailing winter winds and shaded from the summer sun? Do you have access to water, in case of fire? Is there room for building expansion? Is there a flat area, approximately 30'x80', with a slight downhill slope, in case you put in a septic system and drainage field?

6. Future. Check with the town zoning board to learn of any anticipated plans for highway expansion or other major building activity that can affect your land.

7. Noise. Are there any airplane routes overhead or anticipated airports or factories planned for the future?

8. Neighbors. Are there any neighbors that might object to your building near them?

9. Building restrictions. Find out if there are any legal covenants or property association by-laws that might restrict or govern the size or type of structure that you build on your property.

10. Zoning. Does the property have any zoning restrictions? Does zoning allow for commercial endeavors that might lead to future problems and excessive noise, disrupting the very solitude that you built the cabin to obtain?

11. Services. Can fire trucks reach your cabin, in case of fire? This will also affect your insurance rates.

12. Flooding or wetlands. Is the property in a flood plain? Make sure you are not buying land that has been designated a wetlands area.

If the cost of land and the amount of labor involved to build a cabin is too daunting for you, you might consider buying property with another person or couple, sharing the labor and dividing the use of the cabin. This can, of course, be tricky and should not be ventured into lightly.

Another possibility is to put an ad in a local (rural) paper expressing a desire to rent or lease a small piece of land from a farmer or land owner. You would need a legal agreement that you could build a small cabin on it. By renting land, you avoid paying property taxes, commissions, lawyer's fees, closing fees, title searches and surveys. You would, however, have to work out what happens

Selecting a Building Site

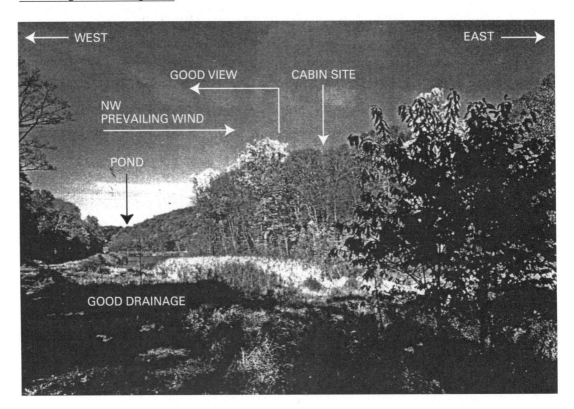

if the farmer sells his land, where access to the cabin would be, and who pays for liability insurance, etc. You might include an option to buy clause, in the leasing contract.

One cabin builder we interviewed had a friend with a large tract of land that he was holding onto for investment purposes. The land owner was happy to have a cabin built on his land, with the understanding that he could occasionally use it.

Another reason for building a cabin is to use it as a temporary shelter until you can afford to build a more substantial weekend or summer house. The original building can then be used as a guest house. This gives you a chance to live on the property, observe the path of the sun, the prevailing winds and the changes in climate before investing in a bigger structure. You may find that a cabin is all you need. Another option might be to build a small cabin and add onto it as your family or income grows.

Access

Depending upon how adventuresome you are, you might not need a road at all. Perhaps a path to your cabin is sufficient to transport materials, using a hand cart with bicycle wheels or a sled in the winter. One of our cabin builder friends carried his supplies up the side of a mountain in Alaska, using a series of ropes as hand holds. Other ways of carrying supplies to your cabin are by floating the material by raft or suspending the material between two canoes. ATVs can be helpful too, or even snowmobiles in the winter. In really remote areas, you might even consider air dropping materials onto your site. Just remember, where there's a will, there's a way.

Road Building

If there is no road leading to your cabin site, you may have to build one. This may not be as difficult as you think, as long as you are willing to take a few days off and help do some of the work. Hire a driver with a front end loader or a large, four-in-one backhoe. The operator should have experience in building roads. You will also need to hire a dump truck with a driver. Meet the front end load driver at your property line and walk over the proposed roadway. Try to avoid any rock outcrops, as these may have to be blasted with dynamite and can be expensive. Mark the route with brightly colored tape. Check with the building department for the road requirements in your area (surface material, width, etc.) and keep in mind that most building codes don't permit a grade of more than 14 degrees.

Begin by clearing a 14' wide swath of trees, to make a path for the front end loader. Also, cut any overhanging branches that might get in the way of a 14' high truck. Check with the local fire department and find out what kind of space they need near your cabin to turn their fire engines around. Cut the trees off 4' from the ground, to give the machine more leverage to pull the stumps out by the roots. If you encounter a steep hill, the front end loader will have to cut-and-fill to level it off. Depending on the length of the road, order enough gravel or other approved surfacing material to spread a 4" layer on the top of the graded road surface. The road should be a minimum of 12' across with a slight crown in the middle, to help shed water.

If your road is traversing diagonally up a hill, as is often the case, you may experience washouts in heavy rains, washing away much of the road. To avoid this, build a French drain. A French drain is a ditch, lined with fist-sized rocks, running diagonally across the road. Water hits the French drain and is diverted to the side of the road, to a run-off area. To make sure the ditch itself doesn't wash away, put a 2x8 pressure-treated board, on edge, in the downhill side of the trench.

French Drain

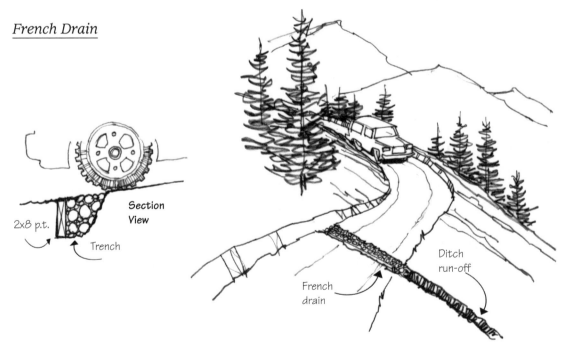

2x8 p.t.

Section
View

Trench

French
drain

Ditch
run-off

Your local highway department may also require you to provide an asphalt apron, with a 15' radius, where your new driveway joins an existing town road. You also may have to provide a small culvert if your road crosses over any wet area. A culvert is a corrugated, galvanized steel pipe that is laid in a trench dug out by a backhoe during the dry season. The culvert is covered with backfill, and the top is finished with the same surface as your road. Before beginning your road building, check that you have all the necessary permits.

Site Planning

Begin by setting 4' long stakes in the ground, located approximately where you think the cabin should sit. Walk around the stakes and try to visualize in your mind's eye how the cabin will look and feel once you are in it. Imagine you are standing in the living room or on the porch, and picture the view from different rooms. Take into consideration the sun and prevailing winds. One cabin builder we know, Ray Sherman, bought land in the Adirondacks. Before building his cabin, he spent time tenting out on the land, waking up to the sun rising behind the White Face mountains and ending the day with the same magic light bouncing off them.

Building Plans

Although some basic cabin plans are included in this book, you may want to alter or expand them to suit your specific requirements. An easy way to draw your own plans is to buy some grid paper with 1/4" squares, from your local stationery store. Assume that each 1/4" square is 1 square foot and use a straightedge or architect's scale to draw your cabin plans.

Once you have a plan that looks right to you, you can make a scale model that will help you visualize it better. This can easily be done by photocopying the plans and gluing them onto a sheet of foam core. Cut the pieces out, using an X-acto or matte knife, and glue them together.

Cabin Reflections

As kids growing up in the early 1940s, we eagerly looked forward to summer vacation from school. We then headed for the Chehalis River, which was located just a few minutes walk from home. There was an island in the river that could be reached in the summer when the water was low by just wading across to it. At the far end was a fairly flat area on higher ground that would make a good cabin site. Soon we were busy chopping down cottonwood trees near the site. It's a·wonder someone did not get hurt. Some of the trees were 12" in diameter and very tall. By the end of the summer, we had built a cabin that was about 7' wide by 11' long, complete with tar paper roof and wood salvaged from driftwood for the floor. Furnishings included a small table, kerosene farm lantern and bunk beds with burlap sacks sewn together with straw filling for the mattresses. A small cookstove with oven was given to us by a neighbor for heating and cooking. The question now was "how do we get it to our cabin?" My building partners, Arthur and Roy, owned a red wagon that we used to get it to the river bank. The river was high this time of year so we had to ferry it across on our makeshift raft. With luck and hard work, we got it to the cabin undamaged. A hole cut in the roof and some stove pipe made the job complete. Potatoes sure tasted good fried on that old stove. The cabin could now be kept warm and cozy on cold days and nights. At night the sound of the rain on the roof soon lulled us off into sleep.

—David Hense

Photo: David Hense

TYPES OF CABIN CONSTRUCTION

For two years I lived alone in the woods in a house which I built myself. I am convinced by experience that to maintain oneself on this earth is not a hardship but a pastime, if we live simply and wisely.

—Thoreau, *Walden*

Log Building

If you live in an area where there are an abundance of tall, very straight trees, this method of construction may be the choice for you. Although the materials are relatively inexpensive, log building is very labor intensive. (A single layer of logs could take a day to cut, notch and install).

An alternative to cutting your own is to buy pre-seasoned, milled logs. No matter whether you buy or cut your own logs, this type of construction is bound to make you proud of the results. See Chapter 4 for more information on building with logs.

Pole Built Cabins

Pole building, one of the first building techniques to be used in many parts of the world, continues to be practical and economical today especially with the advent of pressure-treated poles and more durable fasteners.

There are many advantages to building with poles. Pole buildings resist flooding, hurricanes and earthquakes better than conventional framing. Because it is not necessary to excavate for a foundation and heavy equipment does not have to be brought to the site, pole building has less of an impact on the environment. Also, pole building can result in tremendous savings compared to the cost and labor of building a masonry foundation, especially when you are building on a sloped site. And finally, pole building construction is more fire resistant than conventional framed buildings, because it takes longer to burn through heavy timbers than lightweight stick built construction.

There are some challenges and drawbacks to pole building. Straight, round poles may be difficult to find, depending on where you live. If this is the case, square poles or posts, which are usually available at your local lumber yard, can be used. These are easier to build with and come already pressure treated but are generally limited to 16' lengths. Several deep holes will have to be dug, so make a trial hole before deciding on this type of construction. If your soil is too rocky or filled with clay, this may not be the most practical building technique.

Pole holes can be drilled using an 18" or 24" auger, run off of the back of a tractor. Poles should be spaced between 8' to 12' apart and held together using horizontal, longitudinal beams called girts. These are generally double, 2x10 pressure-treated beams, bolted to each side of each pole. 2x8 or 2x10 floor joists are nailed on top of the girts.

Bury poles as deeply as possible in the ground—a minimum of 36" (more in northern regions with extreme frost). Poles resist being pulled out of the ground as a result of the friction of the earth on the pole's surfaces; therefore, it is important to compact the soil well as you backfill.

Pole Built Cabin

Corner posts

Horizontal beams can be attached to the posts on the inside or on the outside.

Types of Pole Construction

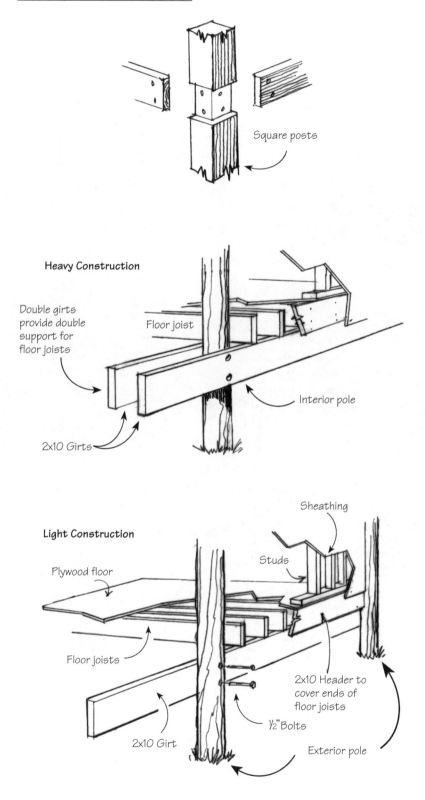

Square posts

Heavy Construction

Double girts
provide double
support for
floor joists

Floor joist

Interior pole

2x10 Girts

Light Construction

Sheathing

Studs

Plywood floor

Floor joists

2x10 Header to
cover ends of
floor joists

½" Bolts

Exterior pole

2x10 Girt

Pole Construction

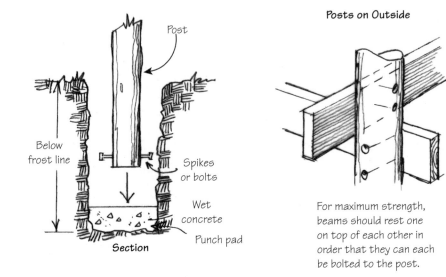

Section

Post

Below frost line

Spikes or bolts

Wet concrete

Punch pad

Posts on Outside

For maximum strength, beams should rest one on top of each other in order that they can each be bolted to the post.

Posts on Inside

Slightly more difficult to frame the walls around the posts

A pole building can be constructed with the poles exposed or with the poles on the interior. Keeping the poles on the outside of the structure eliminates the possibility of toxic fumes from the preservative on some poles from entering the cabin.

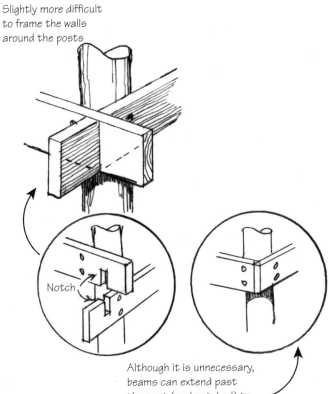

Notch

Although it is unnecessary, beams can extend past the post (and notched) to create a nice appearance. . . or simply joined like this.

Stick Built Cabins

Conventional stick built framing is the method of choice for the majority of builders today. This is because lumber yards stock all the necessary building supplies and because the average carpenter is familiar with dimensional lumber.

First, a masonry foundation is built using either a crawl space or a partial or full cellar. This is covered with a platform comprised of a 3/4" plywood sub-floor, supported by wood joists, spaced 16" on center. This platform will be used as a flat working surface on which to lay out and build the walls before they are tilted up into position. A 2x4 or 2x6 "cap plate" is nailed on top of the walls, overlapping the corners and tying the walls together. Because the walls are fairly light-weight and easy to build, a 14' wall can be built and tilted up by one person, making this type of construction a good choice for a cabin builder working alone.

Stick Built Cabin with Gable Roof

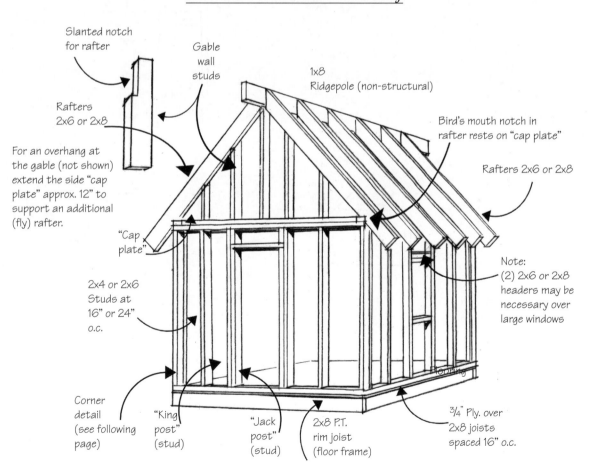

Slanted notch for rafter

Gable wall studs

1x8 Ridgepole (non-structural)

Rafters 2x6 or 2x8

Bird's mouth notch in rafter rests on "cap plate"

For an overhang at the gable (not shown) extend the side "cap plate" approx. 12" to support an additional (fly) rafter.

Rafters 2x6 or 2x8

"Cap plate"

Note: (2) 2x6 or 2x8 headers may be necessary over large windows

2x4 or 2x6 Studs at 16" or 24" o.c.

Corner detail (see following page)

"King post" (stud)

"Jack post" (stud)

2x8 P.T. rim joist (floor frame)

3/4" Ply. over 2x8 joists spaced 16" o.c.

Before you begin, decide whether to use 2x4 or 2x6 studs. 2x4s will save a little money, but 2x6 studs can be spaced 24" apart and give you thicker wall insulation. On the other hand, if you are going to use sheetrock on the interior, you should space the 2x6 studs 16" on center, to give the sheetrock adequate support. Make sure to add a third stud at the end of each wall in order to provide a nailing surface for the edge of the sheet rock. If you are building a gabled or double-pitched roof, install a cross-tie every 4' between the rafters, to prevent the side walls from bowing out under snow load pressures.

Stick Built Details

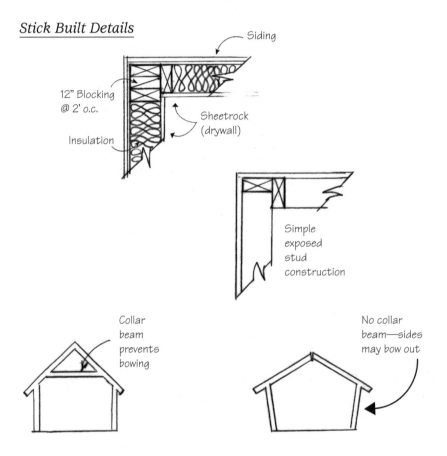

Siding

12" Blocking @ 2' o.c.

Sheetrock (drywall)

Insulation

Simple exposed stud construction

Collar beam prevents bowing

No collar beam—sides may bow out

Post and Beam Cabins

Post and beam construction was used by ancient civilizations to construct stone columns and massive stone lintels, some of which are still standing after 3,000 years.

A more advanced form of post and beam construction is timber framing, which was used by early settlers. It can be recognized by its large timbers and intricate joints. In the early 1800s, saw mills began using circular saw blades which made cutting timbers much more economical. Gradually this led to the wood being cut into smaller pieces (2x4s and 2x6s) and resulted in the more commonly used stick built framing that we see today. Stick built construction requires less-skilled carpenters since the wood is not notched and instead relies on nails to hold it together.

In post and beam construction, simple lap joints (as shown here) are relatively easy to make. The strong structural timbers support the roof without the need for support from the walls. To give the structure lateral support and to help resist the wind, diagonal knee braces are used throughout.

Post and Beam Cabins

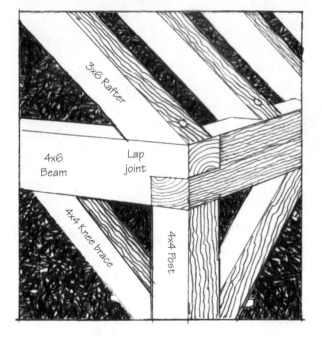
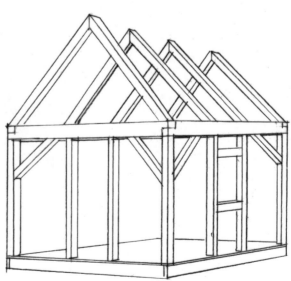

Stone Cabins

If you have ever built a stone wall in your yard or garden, you know the feeling of making something that will last forever. No other building material, including steel, is as durable and permanent as stone. Stone does not rot, swell, contract or burn like wood does and it requires practically no maintenance. We think of stone as the Rolls Royce of building materials, partly because we know how much labor goes into building something out of stone. Among our building projects, our stone fireplace is one of our proudest accomplishments. If you have never worked with stone, before rushing into a full-scale project try building something small, like stone steps or a low wall, to get the feel of it. You may find, as we did, that you need to start out with twice as many stones as you actually use. Unlike bricks or concrete blocks, no two stones are alike and much of your time will be spent looking for stones just the right size and shape to fit together. A few stones may even need to be cut, using a hammer and chisel, in order to fit properly. Allow plenty of time for building a stone cabin—think years, not months. It may take ten times as long to build a stone cabin as a wooden one, but it will last a hundred times longer. Charles McRaven, the author of *Building with Stone and Stonework*, wrote that building with stone "will take a lot out of you and give a lot of satisfaction in return."

Finding proper stone and hauling it to your site can be difficult. Keep an eye out for old buildings being torn down in your area and get permission to remove the stones that are turned up from their foundations. All you need is a pick-up truck, a pry bar, leather gloves and a strong back to recycle them into your new cabin. A second-hand tractor with a front end loader would be a good investment if you are seriously considering building a stone cabin. It can be used to haul rocks, using a stone sled, from nearby fields, and it can prove very useful for lifting stones when working high on a wall.

Masonry mortar, or "mud" as it is called, is different from Portland cement and is used as a filler, not a glue, between stones. The stones must be fitted together (called "dry" stonework) before applying any mortar.

Slip Forms for Building Stone Walls

Another way to build with stone is to use wooden slip forms on both sides of the wall as you build up. This technique is described by the Nearings in *Living the Good Life*. This method uses approximately

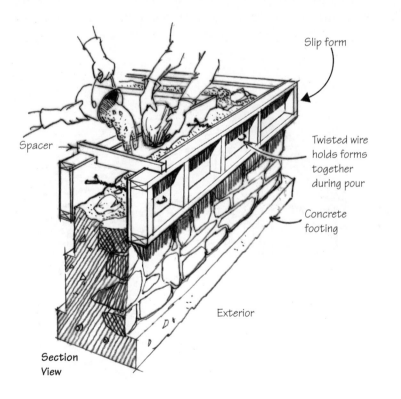

Slip form

Spacer

Twisted wire holds forms together during pour

Concrete footing

Exterior

Section View

equal amounts of concrete and stone and reduces the time required to raise a stone wall. Stones are placed so that they will show on the exterior when the forms are removed.

Because stone walls provide very little insulation, most stone house builders add a 2x4 interior stud wall and Fiberglas batt insulation. In addition to being a poor insulator, stone also sweats a lot when it is cold on the outside and warm on the inside (like the windshield on your car). This can be remedied by placing a sheet of plastic inside the wall cavity, behind the insulation, to act as a vapor barrier.

Cordwood Cabins

Cordwood construction became popular in the 1960s as one way of reducing the cost of materials for do-it-yourself home builders. The drawings illustrate how an 8'x10' cabin can be built out of 5 1/2" thick cordwood/masonry walls, framed with 6x6 timbers. A larger structure would require logs 12" to 16" long with a criblike stacking of logs at the corners.

To make the walls, fill two large garbage pails with sawdust from a local lumber yard or cabinetmaker, and purchase two bags of masonry cement and two bags of lime. Have 2 cubic yards of sand delivered, and you are ready to begin filling the walls.

In a mortar pail, combine 6 parts sand, 6 parts sawdust, 3 parts Portland cement and 2 parts lime. Measuring accurately is critical.

Gradually add water until the mixture has a plastic feel (not too runny and not too stiff and chunky). The sawdust's function is to make the joints more ductile and allow for shrinkage and expansion of the wood. Lay a thick bed of mortar along the bottom plate, and place the logs side by side on top. Fill the spaces between them with at least 1/4" of mortar separating the logs at the closest points. If the space between logs is more than 2 1/2", fill in with a small branch section. Split the logs in half, if necessary, where they meet the side posts, and vary the log sizes as much as possible to produce an interesting effect. To strengthen the wall, hammer nails between the logs that rest against the timbers. To fill thin cracks, hold a large trowel of mortar upside down, sliding the mortar into the crack with a smaller trowel.

Making a wall with log ends is time-consuming, so allow at least one day per side. After 24 hours, spray the wall with a garden hose and brush off any excess mortar with a wire brush. The mortar mix may take several days to harden. For more detailed information on cordwood construction, see *Sheds*, by David Stiles (see Further Reading).

Corner Construction

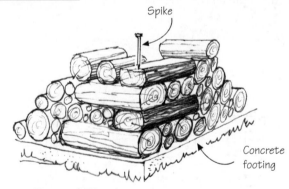

Spike

Concrete footing

Flattened 2' long logs spiked together support corners

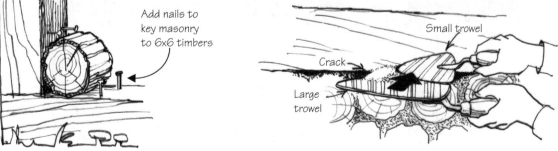

Add nails to key masonry to 6x6 timbers

Cordwood Wall Construction

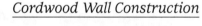

Small trowel

Crack

Large trowel

Wood Siding

When people hear the word cabin, they often picture a log cabin. However as we've seen, cabins can be constructed from a wide range of materials and covered with various types of wood siding. If you decide to use wood siding on the exterior walls of your cabin, there are several types to pick from, including tongue and groove, bevel (clapboard), shiplap, board and batten, slab and plywood.

Bevel (Clapboard)

Bevel siding is a horizontal siding generally made from clear red cedar in 4" to 6" widths. There are two types—plain bevel and rabbeted bevel. The boards are face-nailed at the bottom, using 8d stainless steel nails. Unlike shingles, the nail does not penetrate the previously applied board, and each board is held in place by the board above. Although expensive, this type of siding gives a nice tailored effect to the building. Another variation of horizontal siding that is not beveled is using common 1x8 square-edged boards, overlapping each other by 2". This design requires a "starter" strip at the bottom of the wall to keep the first course pitched out at the same angle as the ones above it.

Bevel Siding

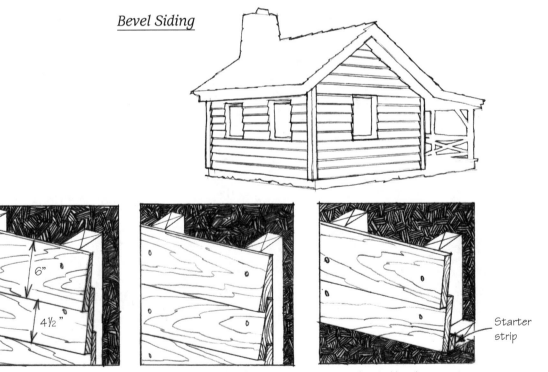

Plain bevel   Rabbeted bevel   Lapped bevel

Tongue and Groove

Tongue and groove siding is usually applied horizontally and is more weathertight than shiplap. It is secured to vertical studs, using only one nail in each stud, driven in at an angle next to the tongue. Using this method, each successive board hides the nail head of the previous board. Tongue and groove siding is generally sold as #2 pine, and is more expensive than shiplap boards but less expensive than bevel (clapboard) siding. It is generally sold in 6" or 8" nominal widths. Tongue and groove siding comes in "V" groove, which accents the joint between the boards by creating a shadow line, or in "center match," which gives the building an almost seamless appearance. Another variation of tongue and groove siding is "drop siding" which is often used in buildings where no sheathing is required, since the joints on the interior are less noticeable.

Tongue and Groove

Tongue and Groove Examples

     "V" groove   Center match

Shiplap

Shiplap siding can be used vertically or horizontally, although vertical seems to be more common. Vertical shiplap siding requires horizontal nailers called "cats," attached every 2' to 3' between studs, on which to nail the siding boards. These nailers not only reinforce the siding, but have the advantage of providing a convenient, built-in shelf on which to store essentials or display woodland or beach treasures. The shiplap boards are generally 8" to 10" wide and are easily nailed to the framing using 8d siding nails. Often, shiplap siding has a rough (undressed) surface on the exterior and a smooth surface on the inside, which results in a thickness slightly less than 1". If you are using the cabin in the winter, insulation and interior paneling are recommended; however, many summer cabins are built with the interior stud framing left exposed. Other variations of shiplap siding which are less commonly

Vertical Shiplap Siding

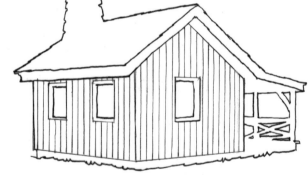

Nailer "cat" stiffens wall

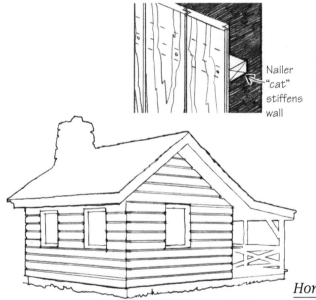

Horizontal Shiplap Siding

Rustic siding

Cabin siding

Faux log siding

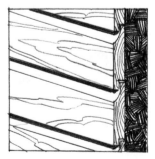

Drop or cove siding

used are: "rustic," "cabin," "faux log" and "drop siding," which is often used on buildings where no sheathing is required, since the joints on the interior are less noticeable.

Board and Batten

Board and batten siding anticipates that boards which are butted together will weather and shrink, leaving a gap between boards that needs to be covered with a batten. Wall boards are held in position by nails placed in the center of each board, allowing the edges to expand or contract. Galvanized 8d (2 1/4") common sinker-head nails are driven through each batten, between the wall boards, and into the nailers. If you are installing siding over 1/2" plywood sheathing, make sure that the nails do not penetrate the plywood completely, unless you are planning to insulate the interior. Board and batten is very commonly used on barns and is a bit less expensive than tongue and groove or shiplap siding, but requires slightly more labor to install.

Board and Batten Siding

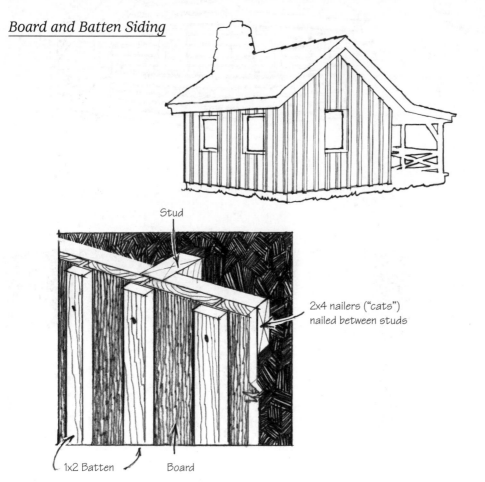

Stud

2x4 nailers ("cats")
nailed between studs

1x2 Batten   Board

Slab Siding

Slab boards are the first or second cuts a saw mill makes when cutting a tree into lumber. Often the outside wood is discarded or sold cheaply. It is not sold at a lumber yard, so you need to purchase this siding directly from a saw mill. You can either order the slab as it comes off the tree, bark and all ("first cut"), or buy the "second cut," leaving bark only on the slab edges. If you opt for the full bark version, you can join the slabs at the corners of the cabin, using vertical logs especially cut into quarters by the saw mill. Take into consideration that after a few years, most bark will begin to peel off the logs.

Slab Siding

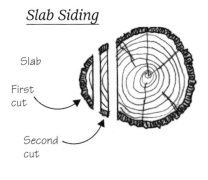

Slab

First cut

Second cut

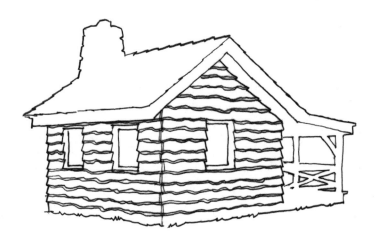

Quarter cut corner log post

Log slabs (first cut)   Log slabs (second cut)

Plywood Siding

Plywood siding has its good and bad points. Good point: the fact that 4x8 sheets of plywood go up very quickly and add strength to the walls. Bad points: there is a lot of waste at the windows, doors and gables, and it is fairly expensive. 5/8" plywood is most often used for exterior siding. It generally comes with 4" or 6" vertical grooves cut into the surface and has a lip (shiplap) along the side, so that each sheet overlaps the previous one.

To save money initially, you can use cheaper 1/2" plywood sheathing to rough in the cabin, and add siding over it later on. Fill any knot holes in the plywood using an autobody cement such as Bondo.

Plywood Siding

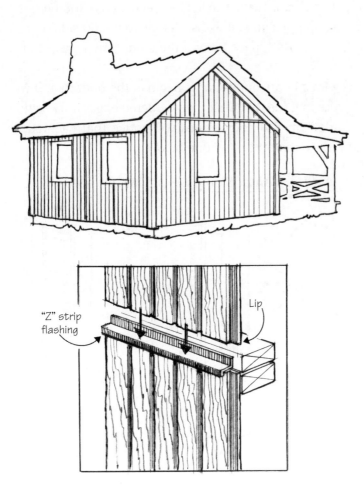

Vertical versus Horizontal Siding

When ordering vertical siding from the lumber yard, insist on exact lengths, not total linear feet. This will reduce both the amount of waste and the labor involved. (This does not apply to horizontal siding, however, since random lengths of lumber can be used to accommodate windows and doors.) We built a barn with 10' high vertical siding on the walls and ordered 10' long boards, thinking we could avoid making any cuts. The lumber company, which was out of "ten footers," delivered 14' lengths, reducing the total quantity of boards, but resulting in the same total linear length. We had to send the boards back and wait two weeks for them to special order our 10' boards.

When joining horizontal pieces of siding, cut the ends of the boards at a 45-degree angle and overlap them, nailing them to the same stud. By beveling the board ends, the joints are less noticeable.

When using stud framing, vertical siding can be supported by horizontal nailers or "cats," nailed between studs. Another less time-consuming option is to nail 1x3 strapping to the outside of the studs, which leaves a 3/4" space behind the studs when viewed from the interior.

As with all horizontal siding, begin at the bottom and work up, making sure that the tongues of the rabbeted edges are positioned so they will deflect, not hold, rainwater. Notice that each successive board overlaps the preceding one below.

Vertical and Horizontal Siding Construction

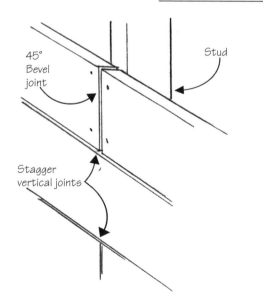
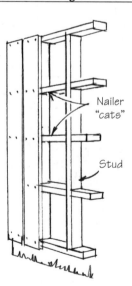
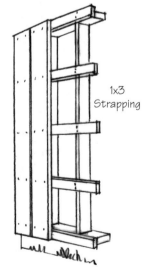

Shingling Over Walls

For a traditional look to your cabin, cover the walls with cedar shingles. Although time-consuming to nail up and rather expensive, they will last a long time.

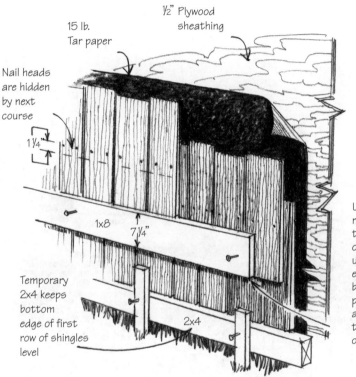

½" Plywood
sheathing

15 lb.
Tar paper

Nail heads
are hidden
by next
course

1¼"

1x8   7¼"

Temporary
2x4 keeps
bottom
edge of first
row of shingles
level

2x4

Use a 1x8 as a guide to
rest the bottom of
the remaining shingles
on while you nail them
up. Placing the bottom
edge of the 1x8 on the
bottom edge of the
previous row of shingles
automatically gives you
the correct exposure
of 7¼".

Cabin Reflections

Patti White built her cabin near the site of the original "Wiener Cabin," built in the 1800s by her great-grandparents. It was a one-room cabin near a spring, behind the family's main house. As each of their children got married, the new couple could live for a year in the cabin off in the woods, "weaning" themselves from living with their parents.

CABIN CONSTRUCTION

I wanted to build. . . with the teeth of the saw, and the explosions of the hammer, and the little shrieks of the screws winding down into their perfect nests.

—Mary Oliver, *Winter Hours*

Along with finding the perfect building site and ordering lumber for your cabin, having the appropriate tools handy for each phase of construction is an essential element in quality, stress-free construction. The key is to plan ahead. There is nothing worse than having to stop in the middle of a job to rush out and buy a tool or material you forgot, especially if you have a crew of friends waiting around to help you build.

Basic Tools

What tools you need will depend on what you are building, but there are a few basic hand tools that are required for most types of construction. The following list contains, in order of importance, the thirteen tools that are most essential.

1. A simple carpenter's pencil. This is indispensable and should always be in your pocket.

These 1/2" wide pencils don't break and are easy to sharpen with a utility knife. They will even mark on wet wood.

2. Tape measure. You will need a 1/2" or 3/4" wide tape measure, at least 16' long. We recommend having two of these on hand (one 16' long and one 25' long), as they are in constant use and are easily misplaced.

3. Measuring tools. A combination square, framing square, 4' level and a chalkline are all essential. Buy good ones. You will be using them often, checking to see if your cabin is square, level, plumb and straight.

4. Hammer. It is a good idea to have two types of hammers: a 20 oz. straight claw hammer for framing and rough work, and a 13 oz. curved claw hammer for fine carpentry. Don't buy cheap hammers with wooden handles as they will eventually break.

5. Hand saw. Even if you are doing most of your cutting using an electric circular saw, you will still need a good hand saw. We recommend the contractor's Stanley Short-Cut saw, which has an aggressive blade that cuts on the forward and the back stroke.

6. Pry bar. This tool is necessary for pulling out nails and correcting mistakes. Also in this category is a 5' long crow bar, useful for digging holes in hard earth and when extra leverage is needed.

7. Clamps. Two 16" bar clamps and a 6' long pipe clamp are the minimum. The pipe for the pipe clamp is sold separately in plumbing supply stores. If you are building smaller items such as furniture, windows and doors, two Jorgenson wood clamps will also come in handy.

8. Chisels. Although you may not be using these a lot, they are absolutely essential in certain situations. It is best to buy a set of three: 1/4", 1/2" and 3/4" which will cover most situations.

9. Rasp. Rasps are designed for removing wood, not for smoothing it. When using a rasp, it may be helpful at first to wear gloves, since one hand has to press down on the end of the tool. A combination rasp and file, called a four-in-hand, is useful for finer work.

10. Utility knife. This handy tool will be used everyday. Order an extra package or two of blades since a sharp knife is a safer knife.

11. Screwdriver. You need one for Phillips and one for slotted head screws—both medium and large size. Even if you plan on using an electric or battery operated screw gun, you will use these often.

12. Wrench. The most commonly used is an adjustable crescent wrench, which is used for turning lag screws and tightening nuts on bolts.

13. Pliers. Several types of pliers may be necessary, especially if you anticipate doing any plumbing or electrical work. A pair of long-handled channel locks are best for working on large objects such as pipes, while a pair of needlenose pliers are good for electrical work. Adjustable vise grip pliers are used for anything that has to be held tight.

Power Tools

Building any project today is a breeze compared to building eighty or ninety years ago. The reason, of course, is power tools. Can you imagine cutting a 16' board lengthwise (ripping) using only a handsaw! What used to take an experienced carpenter eight to ten minutes of backbreaking work takes today's carpenter only seconds, using an electric saw.

Knowing which power tools to buy can be difficult, since there are so many to choose from. These four are the most useful:

1. A portable electric circular saw (sometimes called a skill saw). For large scale building, this worm-gear type circular saw is the tool of choice, although those not accustomed to one might find it heavy at first. If you plan to cut many 4x4s, buy a saw with an 8" blade, which will cut through the wood in one pass. If most of your work is cutting 2x4s, dressed lumber and plywood, a lighter saw with a 6 1/2" blade is less tiring to use.

2. A 3/8" variable speed reversible electric drill. This easy-to-use drill is indispensable for practically every imaginable carpentry job. Gone are the days of slowly boring holes with a brace and bit or setting screws with a hand screwdriver. Because screws hold so much better than nails and are easy to remove in case you make a mistake, we have substituted them for nails in most of our projects. If we had to choose between buying a cordless, battery operated drill or a corded electric drill, we would pick the latter. Cordless tools are great, especially when you are working up in the rafters, where dragging along an extension cord is difficult; however, they always seem to run out of power and need recharging just when you need them. The best solution is to own one of each. Don't forget that you need both twist drill bits and spade (flat) drill bits, as well as a set of Phillips or slotted head screw bits, to go with your drill.

3. A table saw is especially useful if you are making your own windows or furniture. Although not very practical for making cross cuts on long pieces of lumber, the table saw is the tool of choice for making rip cuts (lengthwise) on a board. You can buy portable table saws that are light enough to take to the site, or you can buy floor models and make all your rip cuts in the shop.

4. If you anticipate cutting round corners or irregular shapes you will need a good electric jig saw. Spend enough money to buy the best; the cheaper ones cut poorly and fall apart quickly.

TOOL SAFETY

- Always wear safety glasses when using high-speed power tools.
- Use ear plugs to protect your hearing when you are using high-speed power tools.
- Keep a first-aid kit handy.

Hand Cart

We have found many uses for this easy-to-construct cart, one of which is to move building materials around a job site. The secret of the cart is that the weight of the load is balanced over the wheels, enabling you to easily push heavy loads. David designed the cart long before they were commercially available. He got the idea from the Vietnamese, who transported 500 lb. oil drums on bicycles along the Ho Chi Minh trail. Each of the garden cart wheels is rated at 300 lb. capacity. If not available locally, they can be mail-ordered from the Northern Professional Hydraulics Catalog (see Sources).

Begin this project by ordering the wheels and axle for the cart. Since dimensions may vary, it is advisable to wait until you have received the wheels to determine the exact width. You may have to adjust the width of the cart slightly to accommodate the axle. If you are ordering the wheels, measure the width of the hubs (approximately 3") and add 1/2" onto each end, plus the width of the cart and handles (32"). Using this dimension, have your local metal shop cut a piece of 3/4" diameter

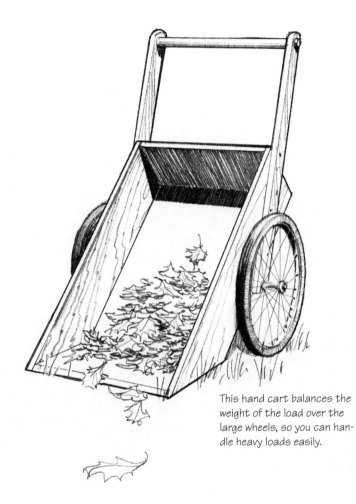

This hand cart balances the
weight of the load over the
large wheels, so you can handle heavy loads easily.

steel rod, with a 1/8" diameter hole drilled 1/4" from the end, for the cot-
ter pin.

Referring to the cutting plan, cut out all the pieces from one 4x8
sheet of 3/4" exterior plywood. For the arms, cut two 48" long pieces
from an 8' long piece of 5/4x4 pressure-treated lumber. Round off the
ends using an electric jig saw, then sand them smooth. Bore a 1 1/2"
diameter hole in the center of each arm, 1 3/4" from the end, and
make a 3/4"x2" notch in the bottom end of each arm where it will
straddle the axle. Fit the 1 1/2" diameter pole (handle) into the hole
at the top of each arm, and secure with a 2" galvanized deck screw.

Assemble the cart box by screwing the sides to the back, front
and bottom, using 2" galvanized deck screws, every 4". Note that the
side pieces overlap the front, back and bottom pieces.

Cutting Plan for Hand Cart

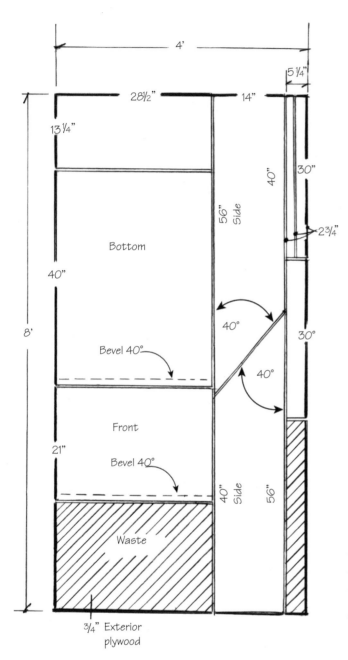

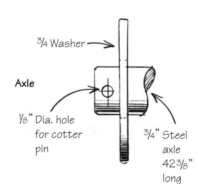

Mount the axle across the bottom of the cart, 20" from the back edge of the cart box. To hold the axle in place, glue and screw two 2 3/8"x30" strips of 3/4" plywood under the bottom of the cart. Position the strips 20" from the back, allowing a 3/4" gap for the axle. Glue and screw a 5 1/4"x30" piece over the two strips, so there is a 3/4"x3/4" opening for the axle.

Fit the two arms over the axle, and screw them to the sides of the cart using six 1 1/2" galvanized deck screws on each side. Pump up the tires and load it up.

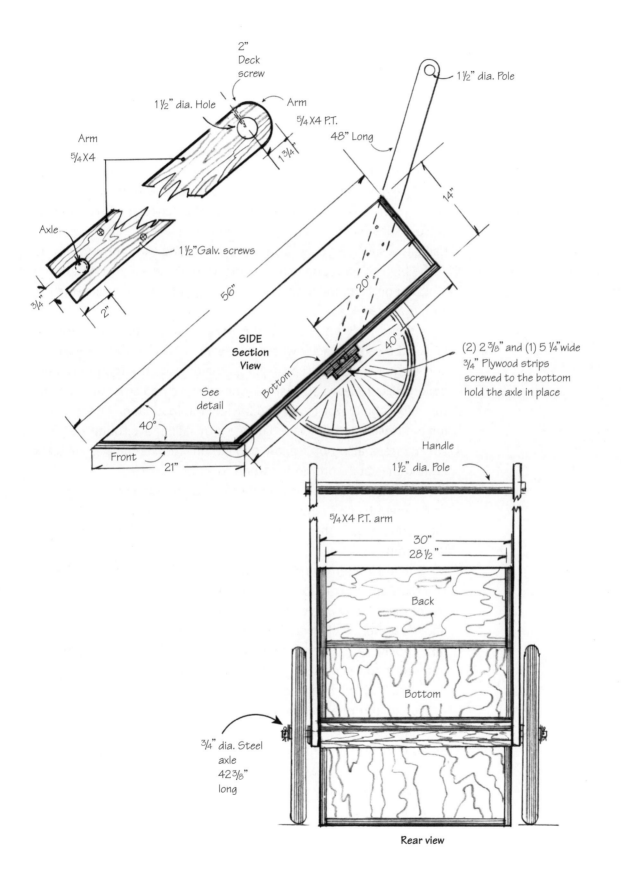

2"
Deck
screw

1½" dia. Hole

Arm
5/4 X4 P.T.

48" Long

1½" dia. Pole

Arm
5/4 X4

1 3/4"

14"

Axle

1½"Galv. screws

3/4"

2"

56"

20"

40"

SIDE
Section
View

Bottom

See
detail

40°

Front

21"

(2) 2 3/8" and (1) 5 1/4"wide
3/4" Plywood strips
screwed to the bottom
hold the axle in place

Handle
1½" dia. Pole

5/4 X4 P.T. arm

30"

28½"

Back

Bottom

3/4" dia. Steel
axle
42 3/8"
long

Rear view

Site Preparation

To lay out the cabin site, begin by setting 4' long stakes in the ground approximately where you think the cabin should be built. Walk around the stakes and try to visualize how the cabin will look and feel once you are in it. Imagine that you are standing in the living room or the outside porch and observe the view at different times of day. Take your time, resetting stakes if necessary until you are sure you have the best location for the cabin. Then choose one corner that you are sure will never change and pound a stake 1' into the ground. Using this stake as your constant, begin staking each corner. Starting at the highest elevation, run a string around the stakes to mark the footprint of the foundation. Use a mason's line level to make sure the strings are level.

Stand back and do a final check, making sure you have positioned the cabin exactly where you want it. Next, remove the string and cut down all the trees inside and alongside the footprint. Most builders like to leave at least 15' on each side of a structure to allow room for a bulldozer to dig and backfill the foundation. Trees standing too close to a cabin can damage it by falling over during a windstorm. Trees also don't allow enough air and sunlight to circulate around the cabin, promoting wood rot.

If you are hiring an excavator to dig a hole for a poured concrete or concrete block foundation, leave the trees cut off 3' to 4' above the ground, to give the backhoe or bulldozer some leverage to pull out the stumps.

If you are removing the stumps by hand, try to chop all the lateral roots and the tap root beneath it with an ax, and pry the stumps out of the ground with a long lever. Cut the wood into 4' long pieces and store them well away from the construction site. Stack the logs in a criblike design to promote seasoning, and later cut the pieces into firewood to be used when the cabin is completed.

Establish an area where the logs or building materials should be delivered, and provide enough room for the delivery trucks to turn around. You might even put up a sign "Leave building materials here" and provide a clipboard nailed to a tree for receipts, notes, etc. When your lumber delivery arrives, check the number and condition of the boards before the driver leaves. Arrange the lumber in piles, with the lumber that is going to be used first nearest the cabin site. It's a good

Removing Stumps

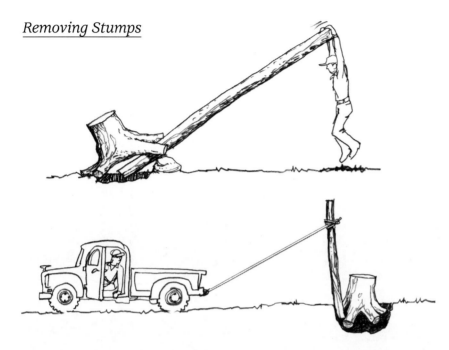

idea to order 5 per cent more lumber than you estimate you will need. This way you can send back any bad pieces back with the next delivery and receive credit. All building materials should be kept off the ground and covered with a tarp. We learned this the hard way when carpenters we hired nailed up some interior cedar boards with clearly visible boot prints on them.

Foundations

Once you have established where your cabin will be situated, you need to set permanent markers that can be periodically checked to determine the exact outside dimensions of the cabin. The traditional way to do this is to set up an elaborate array of batten boards, a time-consuming task and one that wastes valuable lumber. A simpler and quicker way is to set up off-set corner stakes and wrap a yellow mason's line around the posts, marking the perimeter of the cabin. The strings are removed during the construction of the cabin, but any time the foundation walls have to be checked, the strings can be quickly re-strung.

To set the corner stakes, pick a corner of the proposed cabin that you are sure will never change (point #1). Pound a short 2x2 stake in the ground at point #1 and start from here. The difficult part

Placing Stakes

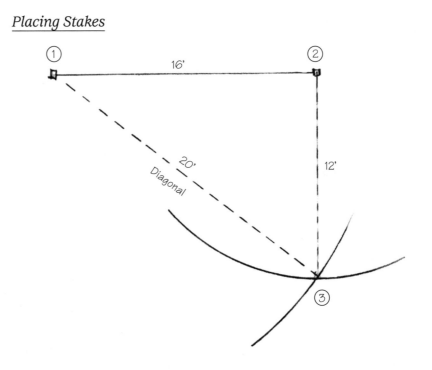

is figuring out how to make the next three stakes exactly perpendicular to each other. The easiest way to do this is to establish the length of the diagonals using the basic formula: $A^2 + B^2 = C^2$.

If, for example, your cabin dimensions are 12'x16', multiply 16' by 16' (256 square feet), multiply 12' by 12' (144 square feet), and add the two totals together (400 square feet). Hit the square root symbol on your calculator and you get the length of the two diagonals (the square root of 400 square feet is 20'). Mark one side of the cabin by measuring over 16' from the first stake, and pound in a second stake. Measure one of the diagonals by using a pointed stick to scribe an arc on the ground, 20' from the first stake, approximately where you think the opposite corner will be located. Scribe another arc, 12' from point #2. Place a stake where the two arcs intersect at point #3. Repeat the same process for point #4 to mark all four corners of your cabin.

One problem with laying out foundations is that the ground may not be level, which could throw off your measurements. A good way to check for level is to use a transit and "shoot" a line. If you don't want to invest in this piece of expensive equipment, an alternative method is to use a cheap $20 infra-red laser pointer, taped to a 4' carpenter's level. Adjust the level so that the bubble is centered in the glass vial and turn on the laser pointer. Hold up a stick where

Cabin Perimeter Markers

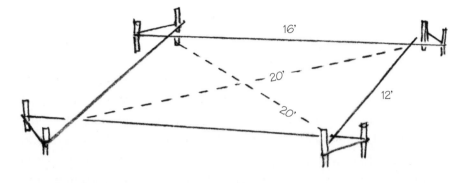

the far corner of the cabin will be and look for the red dot shining on the stick. Subtract the thickness of the level and mark the stick. Do the same for the other three corners.

Setting Perimeter

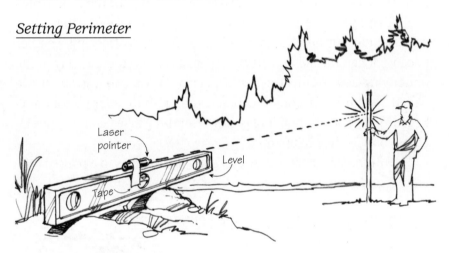

Poured Concrete Foundations

Many small log cabins built years ago are simply resting on a large stone at each corner. Sometimes additional field stones were placed under the sill beams to keep animals from crawling under the cabin and making a home there. When we bought our 120-year-old barn, it had no foundation. The large 6"x8" sill beams were resting on the ground. How these beams resisted rot and insects is still a mystery to us, since we know from experience that there are plenty of termites in the area. When we moved our barn, we placed it on top of concrete blocks to save it from termite infestation and decay.

For a large cabin that is being used year round, a poured concrete foundation may be an option. Poured concrete foundations require forms that are carefully set up on top of previously poured concrete footings. Unless you love mixing and pouring concrete, this is not an easy do-it-yourself project. You can, of course, build the plywood forms yourself and have a transit ready-mix truck deliver the concrete to your site, but the forms themselves are time-consuming to build and set up and there is a substantial waste of lumber when the foundation wall is finished and they are removed. If you are determined to have a poured concrete foundation, you can rent your own forms, but it is often more practical to hire a professional mason for this job and let him worry about the forms blowing out or the mix hardening in the truck.

Poured concrete has other drawbacks, too. This method requires heavy machinery to excavate and then pour the mix, which could damage some of the trees and shrubs near your cabin. Concrete should not be poured or allowed to cure in freezing weather because it can buckle and crack, especially when there is clay in the underlying soil. In most cases, especially if the cabin is small, we would recommend concrete block rather than poured concrete, because the pace of building is slower and mistakes can be corrected as soon as they happen.

Fortunately, there are several good alternatives to a poured concrete foundation.

Formwork for Pouring Concrete Foundation

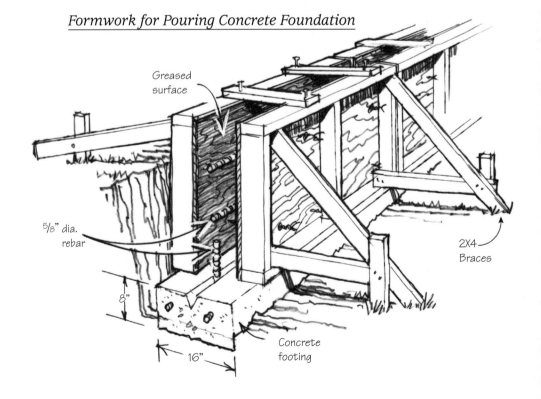

Greased surface

5/8" dia. rebar

2X4 Braces

8"

16"

Concrete footing

Types of Foundations

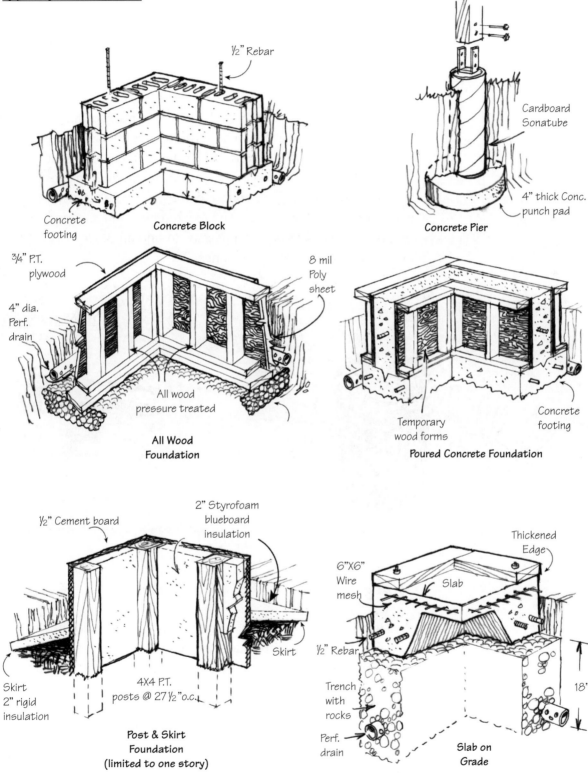

½" Rebar

Concrete footing

Concrete Block

Cardboard Sonatube

4" thick Conc. punch pad

Concrete Pier

3/4" P.T. plywood

4" dia. Perf. drain

8 mil Poly sheet

All wood pressure treated

All Wood Foundation

Temporary wood forms

Concrete footing

Poured Concrete Foundation

½" Cement board

2" Styrofoam blueboard insulation

Skirt

Skirt 2" rigid insulation

4X4 P.T. posts @ 27½" o.c.

Post & Skirt Foundation (limited to one story)

6"X6" Wire mesh

½" Rebar

Trench with rocks

Perf. drain

Slab

Thickened Edge

18"

Slab on Grade

Foundation Posts

Posts or columns have held up structures for centuries, as proven by looking at the Greek Parthenon, the Egyptian temples and the Roman Forum, so they can certainly be used to hold up a small cabin.

Having done some restoration work on old houses in historic East Hampton, Long Island, we have first-hand knowledge of how posts, often made out of locust, have held up houses for over 200 years without rotting. An alternative available today is pressure-treated posts that are rated to last at least forty years. You can extend their life further by covering the bottom of the posts with tar or sealing the ends with wax. However, we still feel the best and cheapest way to support a cabin with wooden posts is to find an old locust tree and to cut it up into the lengths you need.

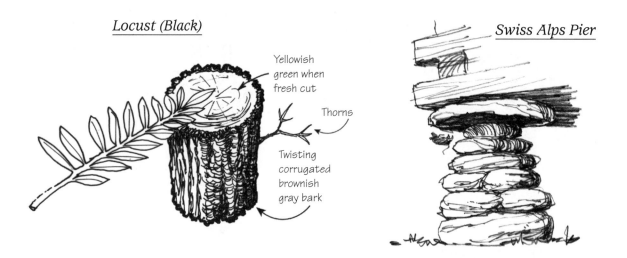

Locust (Black)

Yellowish green when fresh cut

Thorns

Twisting corrugated brownish gray bark

Swiss Alps Pier

Piers

Pier foundations have been used for centuries to hold up wooden houses. The best examples are the typical stone piers used in the Swiss Alps. Swiss cabins typically have a large, flat circular stone at the top of the pier to prevent rats from entering the building.

To construct piers, the builder first digs a hole in the ground 12" below the frost line and fills it with rocks. Sometimes cement is used between the rocks. The stone piers are built on top of the supporting rocks.

Simple Piers

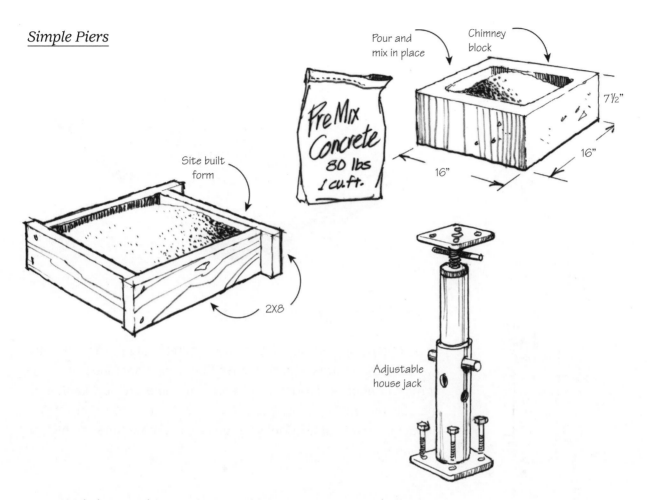

With large cabins, it is sometimes necessary to place piers under the cabin rather than just at the corners to support heavy girders, which in turn support the floor joists. These piers can be as simple as a pile of stones and mortar or concrete blocks; however, some building codes require solid concrete piers. Adjustable house jacks can be used in situations where a cabin may settle (often the case with log cabins). As the cabin settles, these house jacks can be screwed up to compensate for the change in height.

Interior Piers

An easy way to construct interior piers is to build a footing form, using 2x8s, or buy 16"x16" pre-cast chimney blocks which can be used as forms. Position them underneath the girders, fill them with pre-mixed concrete, and mix with water. Interior piers are not affected by frost heave and therefore do not need to go below the frost line.

Interior Piers

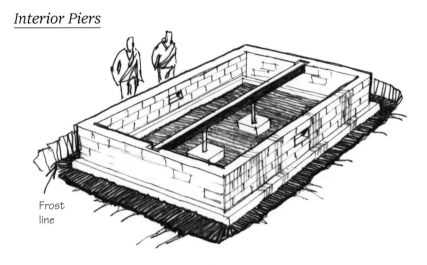

Frost
line

Cast Concrete Columns

Another type of pier support is a cast concrete column. You can easily cast these round columns yourself by using Sonatubes, available at most lumber yards. The thick cardboard tubes are peeled off after the concrete inside them has cured. These tubes come in varying diameters and lengths. Choose a tube that is three times as high as its diameter.

*Cardboard Sonatube
Filled with Concrete*

Drilling in Bedrock

If your cabin site is on bedrock, you can use an electric hammer drill to drill an 8" deep hole into the rock. Cement a 1/2"x12" anchor bolt into the hole. One way to anchor a concrete pier to bedrock is to use a plastic bucket as a form. Place the bucket upside-down over the bolt, leveling the bottom of the upside down bucket with stiff mortar, making sure there are no gaps. Allow the mortar to harden and then pour wet concrete through a hole cut into the top of the bucket. Remove the bucket when the pier has hardened.

Posts can also be attached to the bedrock by cementing a 1/2" eye bolt into the hole. Drill a 1 1/2" hole into the bottom of the post and drop the post over the eye bolt. Secure the post to the eye bolt by inserting a 1/2" diameter lag screw through the eye of the eye bolt. This makes it possible to move the cabin at a later date without cutting the posts, by removing the lag screws.

Anchoring a Concrete Pier to Bedrock

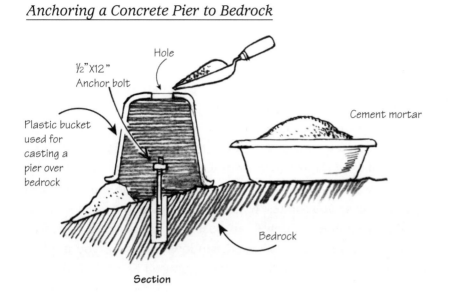

½"X12"
Anchor bolt

Hole

Cement mortar

Plastic bucket
used for
casting a
pier over
bedrock

Bedrock

Section

Attaching Posts to Bedrock

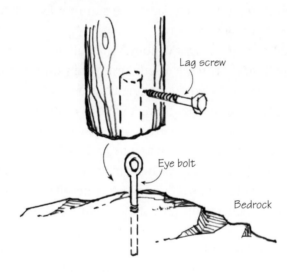

Lag screw

Eye bolt

Bedrock

Windows and Doors

Don't underestimate the importance of having enough windows in your cabin. Windows allow natural light to enter a cabin; without them, a cabin can be a dark and dreary place. Windows enable the cabin dweller to look outside and take in the seasons and surrounding environment.

Windows welcome you in to a warm hearth and a hearty meal. On the other hand, windows and doors can be a source of drafts and cold air, so some planning and foresight is required to make them as air-tight as possible.

Standard double hung, awning or casement-type windows can be ordered and bought at your lumber yard and come complete and ready to install in a rough opening. Just remember that a small 3/16" clearance is already provided for, so that your window will fit into your rough opening with room to spare. If you are buying standard factory-built windows, it is a good idea to have them at the job site before you begin framing so you can test fit them as you build the walls.

Factory-made windows can cost from $150 to as much as $4,000. Second-hand or salvaged windows can save you a lot of money. We once bought a second-hand, unused French window for $300 that the original owner had paid over $3,000 for, and installed it in a garden house we were building, making it unique while affordable. For those concerned about heat loss, factory-made windows come with double-pane or even triple-pane insulated glass, and low "E" glass which restricts the heat in the summer as well as preventing heat loss in the winter.

High-efficiency, air-tight windows may not be necessary for the average cabin that is primarily used during the summer months, and much money can be saved by making your own windows.

European Recessed Window

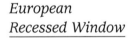

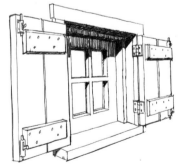

For years, we have been trying to find a solution to the high cost of windows. We started out buying "barn sashes" from the Sears catalog which, back in the 1960s, cost as little as $20. Today, the same window sash (no longer available from Sears) costs $150 and still requires that the owner build a frame around it before installing it. We finally discovered a window, built at the turn of the century, in the attic of a house David was working on. It was perfect in its simplicity. The beauty of it was that it could be easily removed for cleaning, painting or maintenance and, at the same time, it was securely held in place by a simple window transom latch. The window could be opened to any degree just by adjusting the length of a small chain. Because of its unique and simple design, it can even be left open during the rain. We have adapted this design so that although the window appears to be made up of four separate panes, it actually consists of only one piece of 1/8" glass or Plexiglas, with muntins attached to the outside of the glass. This makes the building and installation process much simpler and the window easier to clean. Another thing we like about this design is that it is recessed

Easy-to-Make Tilt-In Window

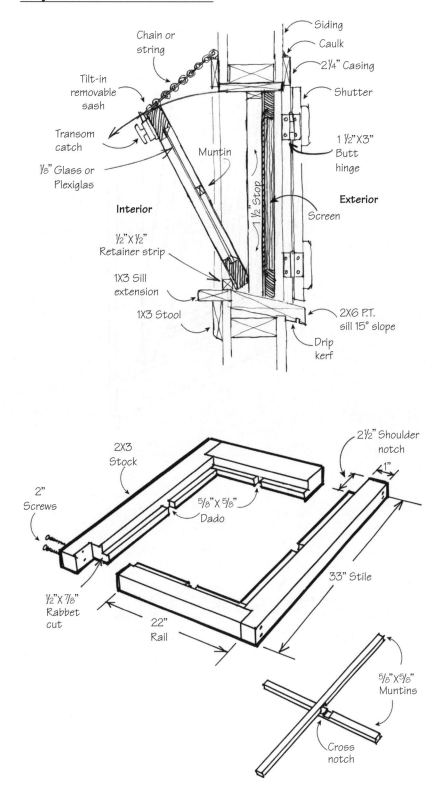

Tilt-In Window

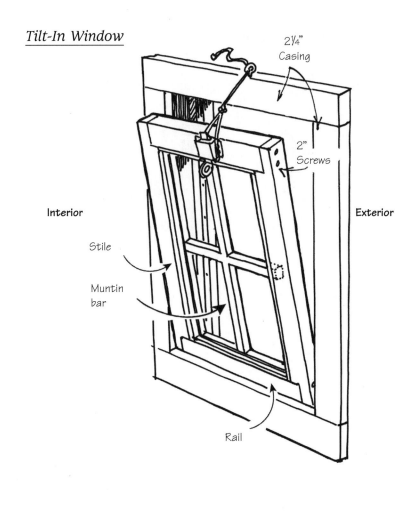

2¼"
Casing

2"
Screws

Interior

Exterior

Stile

Muntin
bar

Rail

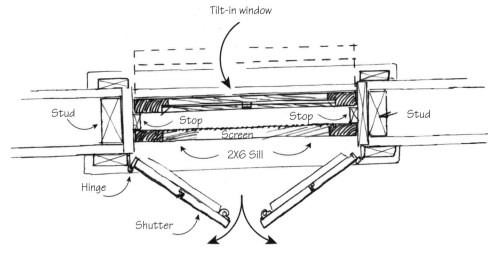

Tilt-in window

Stud

Stop

Stop

Stud

Screen

2X6 Sill

Hinge

Shutter

Plan View

from the front face of the building, giving it the appealing look of many traditional farmhouses in Europe. This recess not only gives the window a shadow line, but it also protects it from the weather.

Homemade Screens

There are very few parts of the country that don't have mosquitoes, especially during hot months of the year and rainy weather. Cabins, often situated near lakes or streams, are especially vulnerable and screens are an important priority. Windows are most often designed to have screens on the outside of the window, since they are less likely to be opened or closed than the windows.

Screens can be simply made by stapling a roll of screening to the top of the window frame and stapling a 3/8"x1/4"x 3/4" stick to the bottom of the screening. In the summer, the stick secures the screen to the bottom of the window opening, and is held in place by

Rolled Screen

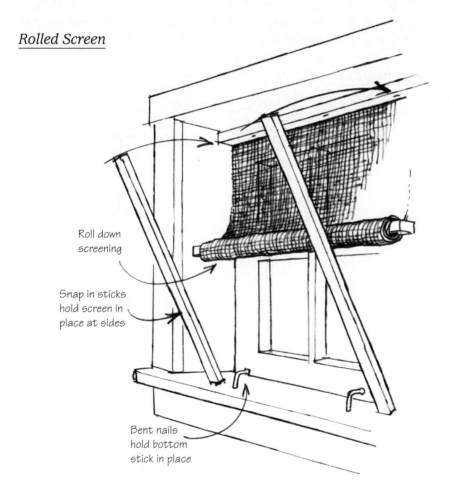

Roll down screening

Snap in sticks hold screen in place at sides

Bent nails hold bottom stick in place

two bent nails. In the winter, when you don't need the screen, you can roll it up and secure it at the top of the window opening. Measure the screening so that it will fit the opening, allowing a little extra screen at the bottom where the stick is attached. Cut the stick a fraction of an inch longer than the distance between the two side window frames. This allows you to bend the stick slightly or spring load it in place during the winter. Cut two additional sticks, just long enough to fit on top of the screen at each side and snap them into place, securing the screen in place. During fluctuations in humidity and temperature, a simple matchbook cover can be used as a shim to compensate for any swelling or expanding of wood.

For a more substantial screen, you can make your own by buying lightweight 1x3 boards (preferably red cedar) and joining the pieces together at the corners with lap joints, brads and glue. Using a table saw, cut a 1/8" wide, 1/4" deep dado groove, 3/8" from the inside edge of all four pieces. Join the pieces together, using galvanized brads and waterproof glue. Once the glue has dried, cut a piece of insect screening 1" larger (on all four sides) than the inside opening. Lay the screening over the frame and, using a tool made especially for this purpose, press the

Homemade Screen

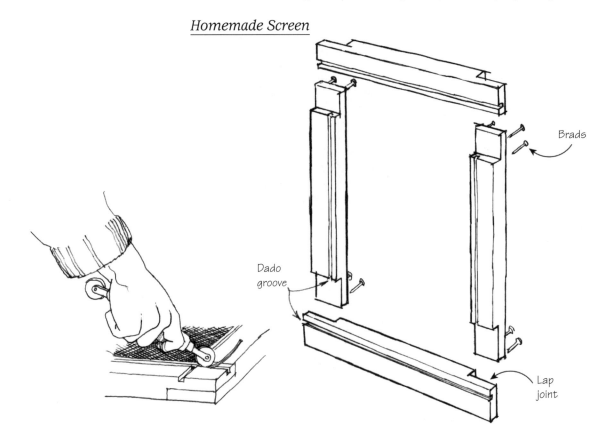

Brads

Dado groove

Lap joint

screen and a special flexible rope, called a screen retaining spline into the groove. Do the top and one side of the frame first. The installation tool and retaining spline are sold in most hardware stores. Cut off any excess screening with a utility knife.

Shutters

Most shutters on houses in North America are purely decorative and serve no purpose whatsoever. They are often, in fact, screwed permanently to the outside walls of the house. In Europe, especially in hot climates, shutters are often practical. They can be partially closed, lending privacy and stopping harsh sun rays from entering during the heat of the day, while the louvers can be left open, allowing cool breezes to enter. Shutters on a cabin can serve many purposes. They can be shut to help keep out the cold on winter nights, and they can

Sliding Window Shutters

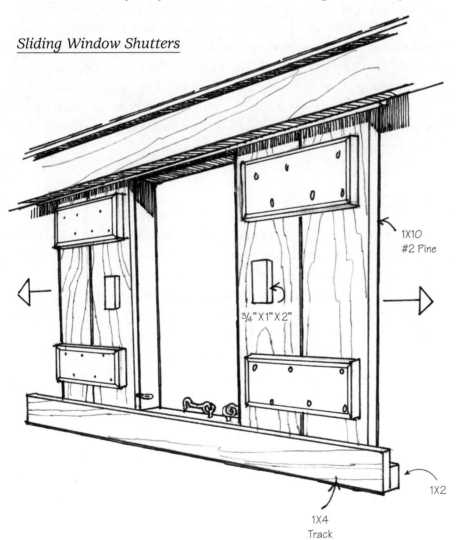

1X10
#2 Pine

3/4" X 1" X 2"

1X2

1X4
Track

also be closed and locked when a cabin is not in use, helping to keep vandals out. Shutters can be installed to swing or slide on a track.

Doors

Doors for cabins built using conventional framing, such as the Lakeside Cabin (see Chapter 5), can be bought or ordered pre-cut at your local lumber yard. This means they come as a complete package, already hinged, bored for your lockset and ready to pop into the rough opening in your cabin framing. A gap of about 1/4" is allowed for shimming the door in place and a door can be installed in less than an hour. The convenience of installation is off-set by the high price you will have to pay for these doors and the fact that they might not have the cabin look you want.

A good alternative is to design and make your own doors. This allows you the freedom of matching the door to your cabin's style and gives it a personal touch. In addition, you will save money on materials. Allow a day to make the door and a day for hanging it and installing hardware. The following typical cabin door can easily be made using common tools. Most exterior doors are 36" wide and most interior doors are 30" wide, with the exception of a bathroom door which sometimes measures 24" in width. Most building codes require that doors be 6'8" (or 80") in height.

Exterior Doors

All doors on the exterior of your cabin should swing outwards, not inwards as on conventional houses. There are several reasons for this: The first is, as the wind blows, the door will press against the cabin, closing any air gaps. Also, anybody trying to break in will be pushing against the frame of the cabin door, as opposed to pushing against a weak 1/2" thick lock mortise. Finally, if the door is built on the outside of the cabin, it can be installed to hang below the sill, preventing rainwater from creeping in. Use non-removable fixed-pin hinges for an extra sturdy door. To avoid a problem with the door hitting the door casing, preventing the door from swinging all the way open and forcing the hinge screws to pull out, increase the width of the hinge, allowing the door to clear the casing. To keep the door from swinging with the wind when it is in the open, install a hook and eye to the door and to the outside wall of the cabin.

Exterior Door Construction

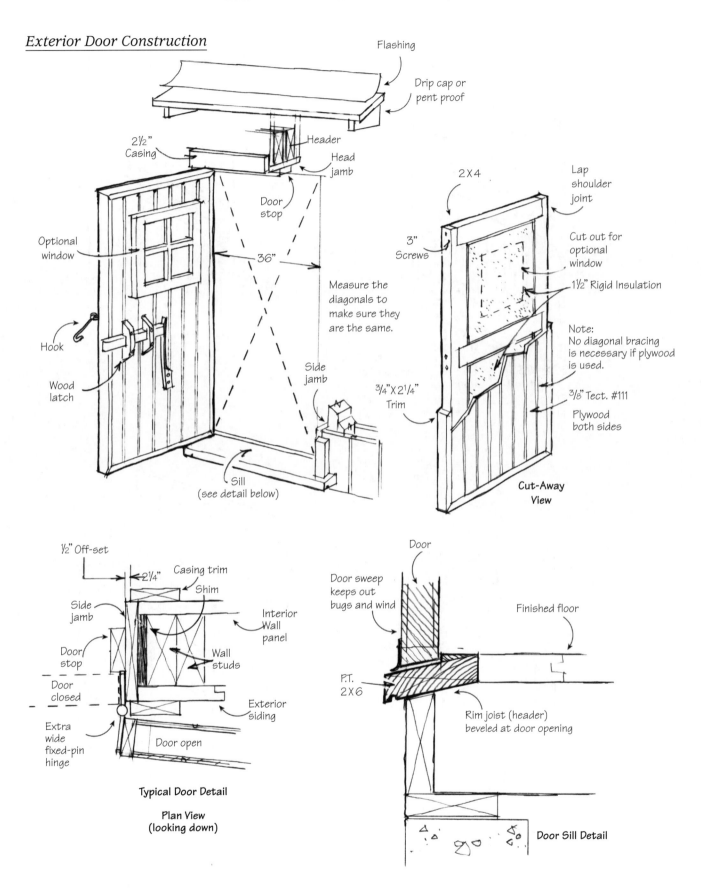

Flashing

Drip cap or pent proof

2½" Casing

Header

Head jamb

Door stop

Optional window

36"

Measure the diagonals to make sure they are the same.

Hook

Wood latch

Side jamb

¾" X 2¼" Trim

Sill (see detail below)

2 X 4

3" Screws

Lap shoulder joint

Cut out for optional window

1½" Rigid Insulation

Note: No diagonal bracing is necessary if plywood is used.

⅜" Tect. #111

Plywood both sides

Cut-Away View

½" Off-set

2¼"

Casing trim

Shim

Side jamb

Interior Wall panel

Door stop

Wall studs

Door closed

Exterior siding

Extra wide fixed-pin hinge

Door open

Typical Door Detail

Plan View (looking down)

Door

Door sweep keeps out bugs and wind

Finished floor

P.T. 2 X 6

Rim joist (header) beveled at door opening

Door Sill Detail

Exterior Door Construction

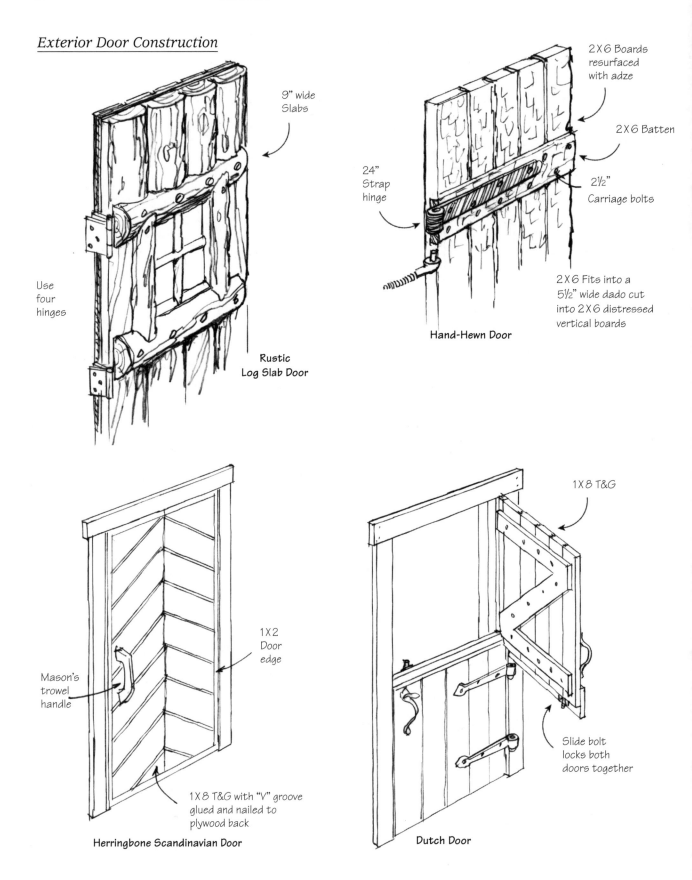

9" wide Slabs

Use four hinges

Rustic Log Slab Door

2 X 6 Boards resurfaced with adze

2 X 6 Batten

24" Strap hinge

2½" Carriage bolts

2 X 6 Fits into a 5½" wide dado cut into 2 X 6 distressed vertical boards

Hand-Hewn Door

Mason's trowel handle

1 X 2 Door edge

1 X 8 T&G with "V" groove glued and nailed to plywood back

Herringbone Scandinavian Door

1 X 8 T&G

Slide bolt locks both doors together

Dutch Door

When you buy a set of hinges for a door, throw away the screws that come with it and substitute 2 1/2" stainless steel screws, making sure that the screws penetrate the heavy framing behind the lightweight door jamb.

A door sill receives a lot of wear and is prone to rot, so make your sill out of pressure-treated 2x6 lumber. Provide a short lip for the back of the door to rest against and make the top flush with the finished floor, so you can easily sweep out your cabin.

A real estate broker once told us that the most important thing to fix up when selling a house is the front entrance, because it is the first impression that makes the difference to the buyer. Some door designs seem to welcome visitors, while others (especially those with an "X" shaped batten crossing the front) subliminally say "keep out." Thus, decisions such as whether you want a window in your door should be carefully considered.

Exterior doors should be at least 1 1/2" thick and can have an interior core of rigid insulation to shield the cabin from the cold. For a log cabin look, you might build a door using log slabs, glued and nailed to a piece of 3/8" plywood. Make your handle out of a crooked piece of branch found in the woods.

For a more rustic look, you can give the impression that you have hand-hewn planks from the forest by buying extra thick lumber, and chipping or distressing the top surface with an adze. Some timber framers think they can achieve the same effect using a portable electric plane, but you can always tell the difference because the chips look too consistent.

Interior Doors

Interior doors can be lighter in weight. They are often constructed out of tongue and groove 1x8 boards with a "Z" shaped brace, made out of heavier 5/4x6 boards, screwed to the back. To prevent the door from sagging, make sure the diagonal brace runs from the top outside cross batten to the bottom inside batten (towards the bottom hinge). This is on the list of questions that we ask carpenters before we hire them. Any door made up of several pieces like this will expand and contract due to seasonal changes, so allow at least 1/8" clearance on all sides. This door lends itself to a simple wooden slide bolt.

Interior Door Construction

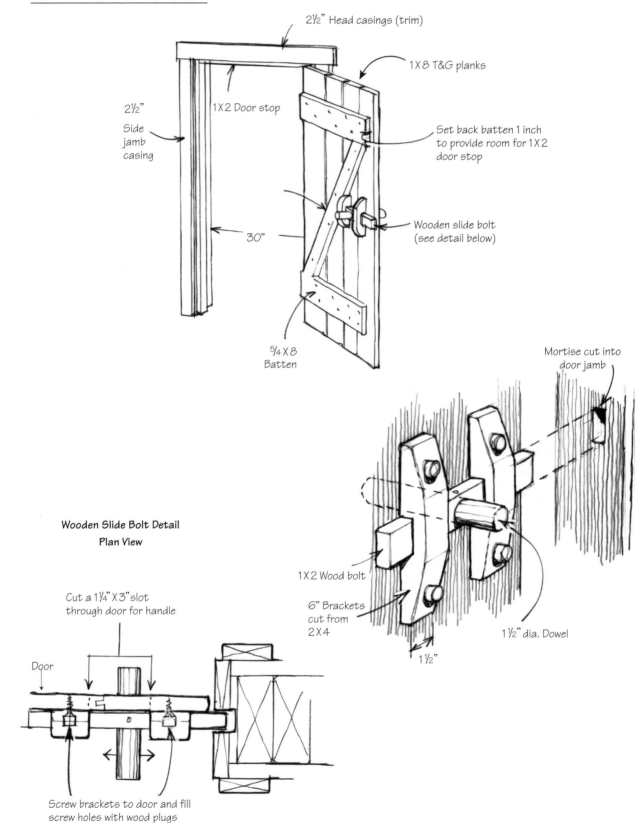

2½" Head casings (trim)

1 X 8 T&G planks

2½"
Side
jamb
casing

1 X 2 Door stop

Set back batten 1 inch
to provide room for 1 X 2
door stop

30"

Wooden slide bolt
(see detail below)

⁵⁄₄ X 8
Batten

Mortise cut into
door jamb

1 X 2 Wood bolt

6" Brackets
cut from
2 X 4

1½"

1½" dia. Dowel

Wooden Slide Bolt Detail
Plan View

Cut a 1¼" X 3" slot
through door for handle

Door

Screw brackets to door and fill
screw holes with wood plugs

Ladders and Stairs

A sturdy ladder is not only useful during construction, but can later be used to access a sleeping loft in your cabin. If you feel that an aluminum ladder would not be appropriate in a rustic cabin, then consider making your own ladder out of logs.

Ladder Construction

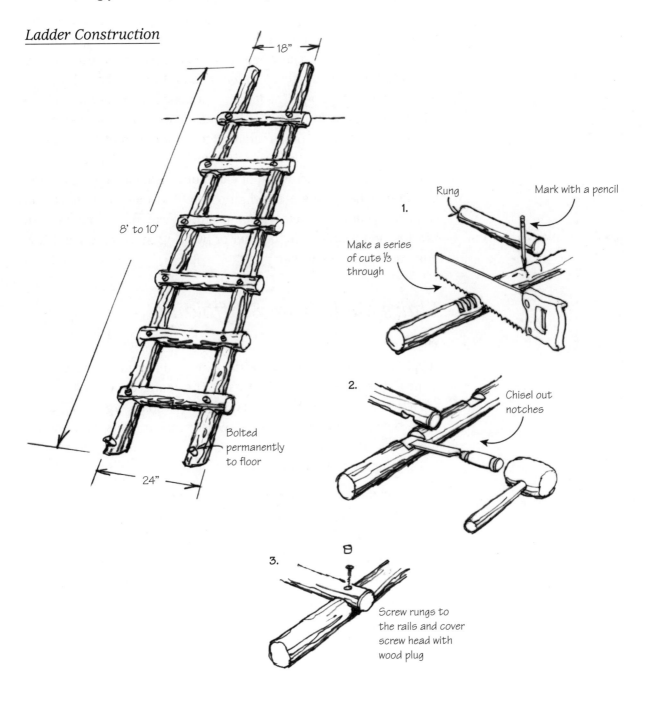

18"

8' to 10'

24"

Bolted permanently to floor

Rung

Mark with a pencil

1.

Make a series of cuts ⅓ through

2.

Chisel out notches

3.

Screw rungs to the rails and cover screw head with wood plug

The design for this ladder is a copy of a ladder we saw in an authentic reconstruction of a pioneer cabin in Williamstown, Massachusetts, with the exception that we use screws instead of pegs. (Note: Unlike most ladders, this one is designed to be used only with the rungs facing you; therefore, it is best if you install it permanently where you are going to use it by nailing it to the floor.)

Find two straight saplings in the woods, approximately 4" in diameter at the bottom end and 3" in diameter at the top end and cut them to the desired length. Cedar is best, but any lightweight species of wood will do. You can often find cedar posts in nursery supply stores in 8' to 10' lengths. You will need a third sapling, 2 1/2" in diameter, for the rungs. The ladder will measure 18" at the top and 24" at the bottom. The distance between ladder rungs is determined by who is using it—approximately 8" for children and 12" for adults. Mark where each rung will meet the long rails (stiles) and carefully make a notch the exact width of each rung, using a hand saw. Chop out the notches, using a chisel, and join the rungs to the rails. You can cheat a little to make the joints stronger by mixing epoxy with sawdust and gluing them together or by using short screws and covering the screw heads with pegs.

Stairs Made from Scaffolding

These stairs are made from scaffolding boards, sold in most lumber supply yards. These boards measure a full 2" thick and 9" wide, which is the size required by code for treads. The boards come 13' long and are rough cut, making them perfect for rustic cabins. It generally takes three boards to build the stairs—two for the stringers, and one for the treads. In addition, you will need two 1x4 boards, approximately 12' long, for the support cleats.

1. To build the stairs, first measure the distance from the first floor to the second floor ("A"), which in our case is 8'10" (or 106", a typical floor height).

2. Divide the total height "A" by 7 1/2" (typical riser height) to find the number of treads (14.13) you will need. Since this must be a whole number, round it down to 14 treads.

3. Multiply the number of treads by 8" to determine "B," which is the distance from the wall to the front edge of the stringer (in this

example, 112"). The reason you use 8" instead of 9" is because the treads have an overhang of approximately 1".

4. Use the Pythagorean theorem to figure out how long each stringer ("C") should be: $A^2 + B^2 = C^2$, and then find the square root of C^2. For example: 11,236" plus 12,544" = 23,780". The square root of 23,780 equals 154.2".

5. To determine the distance between the top edge of each tread, divide "C" (154.2") by the number of treads (14), which equals 11". Measure and mark 11" increments on the front edge of each stringer.

6. Cut the angle at the top and bottom of the stringers by using the dimensions "A," "B" and "C" to form a triangle on a piece of cardboard. Cut out the triangle and use it as a template to mark and cut 26 pieces of 1x4 at an angle, to fit under each tread.

7. Using 3/8"x6" lag screws, attach the stringers to the wall header and the floor. Starting at the bottom, nail the first two support cleats to the inside of the stringers and nail the tread in place. Continue the same process until you reach the top of the stairs.

Scaffolding Stairs

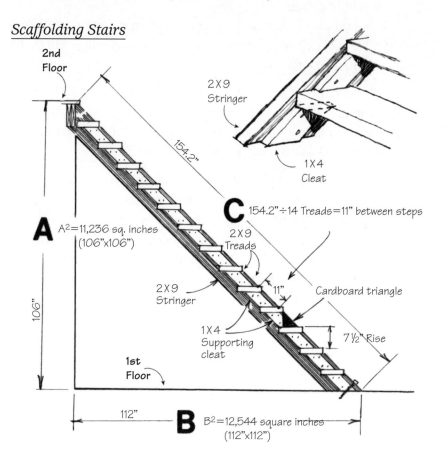

Log Stairs

If you want to build a staircase that will serve as the focal point of your cabin, as we did, be prepared to invest some time in building a set of stairs out of two 10' to 12' long white oak logs Find two logs, preferably white oak, approximately 14" in diameter at the base, tapering to 12" in diameter at the top end. Choose logs without knots so they will split easily. Use one log for the two stringers and the other one for the staircase treads. Split each log in half, starting at the butt end, using a steel wedge and a sledge hammer to make the first opening. As the wood begins to split open, drive in a second steel wedge. To hold the gap open, insert short wooden wedges, called "gluts," you can make yourself by sharpening short pieces of logs. Continue driving wedges along the log until it splits open into two pieces. Using a chain saw and a broad ax, hew a flat surface on both sides of each half. After making the stringers, cut the steps (treads) in the same manner. Decide on how many steps you will need and what width is practical for your cabin. We suggest a stair width between 3' and 4'. Use a chain saw to flatten the top surface of the steps and smooth them off with a plane.

To set up the stairs, follow the procedure mentioned on the preceding page in "scaffolding stairs," marking the angles and where the treads will be placed.

1. Notch out underneath each end of each tread, leaving 2 1/2" thick ends, which fit into 2 1/2" notches in the riser. Each notch should be custom-made to fit each step. We found that an electric chain saw was the easiest tool for this operation.

2. To hold the steps in place once they are in the correct position, drill a 3/4" diameter hole through the top edge of the riser, through the step and into the main body of the riser. Drive a 3/4" hand-carved, oak peg into the two pieces. This locks the tread in and keeps it from rocking. Use epoxy mixed with sawdust to fill any gaps. We made the railing for our staircase from a cedar post and an old barn timber.

Building a Log Staircase

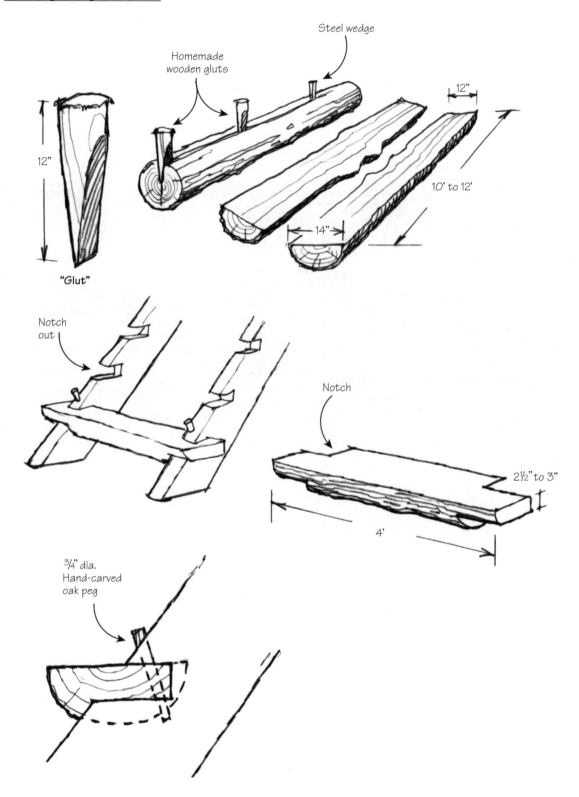

Steel wedge

Homemade
wooden gluts

12"

"Glut"

12"

10' to 12'

14"

Notch
out

Notch

2½" to 3"

4'

¾" dia.
Hand-carved
oak peg

LADDER SAFETY

According to the National Building Association, falling off roofs and ladders is one of the greatest hazards a builder encounters. The following tips should help make ladder climbing safer:

NO   YES   NO

NO

Fulcrum Point

- Make sure your ladder is level to the ground.
- Always face your ladder towards the building—never position it sideways.
- Don't carry anything when stepping from a roof to a ladder—keep your hands free for climbing. (Here's where a tool belt can come in handy.)
- Never leave tools on top of a stepladder where you can't see them from the ground.
- Never step on a ladder rung that is above the resting point of the ladder. This can put your weight on the other side of the fulcrum, making the ladder flip out from under you.

Insulation and Roofing

Insulation

Early settlers realized the importance of insulation and would often stuff their walls with seaweed or hay. Today our energy-efficient homes are mandated by energy codes based on the thermal resistance of building materials, expressed as an "R" value. The higher the "R" value, the better the insulation qualities.

The three most commonly used types of insulation are loose fill, rigid and Fiberglas blanket insulation. The amount of insulation required by your local building department varies according to your climate zone—southern, temperate or northern. If you live on the borderline between two zones, it is best to check with your building department. Determine what "R" value is required in your area, then decide whether you need 2x4 or 2x6 studs to provide space for the insulation. You will also need to size your rafters to meet the required thickness of insulation in the ceiling of your cabin. Allow an additional 1" for air space above the insulation, to keep any trapped moisture from rotting out the ceiling.

Loose Fill Insulation

Cellulose and vermiculite are often used when restoring old houses where getting insulation into small, difficult to reach places is a problem. To accomplish this, 2" holes are bored into the house from the outside, and popcorn-size insulation is blown into cavities between the studs and rafters.

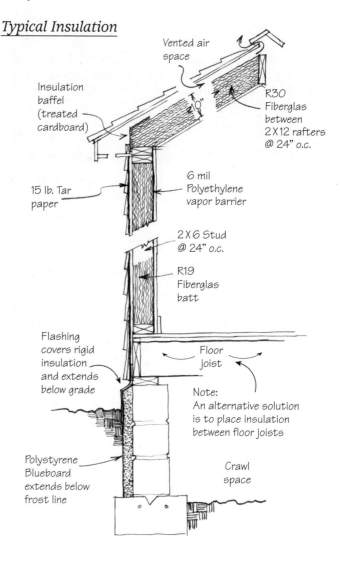

Typical Insulation

Vented air space

Insulation baffel (treated cardboard)

10"

R30 Fiberglas between 2 X 12 rafters @ 24" o.c.

6 mil Polyethylene vapor barrier

15 lb. Tar paper

2 X 6 Stud @ 24" o.c.

R19 Fiberglas batt

Flashing covers rigid insulation and extends below grade

Floor joist

Note: An alternative solution is to place insulation between floor joists

Polystyrene Blueboard extends below frost line

Crawl space

Rigid Insulation

Rigid insulation, such as blueboard (Styrofoam) or pinkboard, is made from extruded polystyrene. These closed cell foams have twice the amount of resistance to heat loss per inch as Fiberglas wool. Rigid insulation is often used underground to insulate foundations since it is impervious to moisture and easy to install. It must, however, be protected from the sun, which will biodegrade it in time. Rigid insulation comes in different thicknesses, ranging from 1/2" to 3", can be covered with reflective foil and is usually sold in 2x8 panels with interlocking tongue and groove edges.

Fiberglas Blanket Insulation

Fiberglas wool blankets and batts are made in sizes to fit between 16" or 24" studs, joists or rafters. A flange on each side is folded out and stapled to the studs. At the top and bottom of each strip, the Fiberglas wool is pulled back, allowing 1 1/2" of backing paper or foil to be stapled to the top and bottom plates. Cut the Fiberglas rolls, using a utility knife and a metal straightedge. Cut through the top foil or kraft paper face, with the Fiberglas wool face down on the floor, compressing the roll with a straightedge. To prevent the microscopic fibers from getting into your skin, cover your hands and arms and wear a respirator to protect your lungs. After you have cleaned up, take a cool shower (not a hot one, as that would open up your pores).

Vapor Barriers and Housewraps

To keep moisture caused by cooking and hot water use inside your cabin from penetrating the walls and causing the insulation to lose its effectiveness, cover the interior walls and ceiling with 6 mil polyethylene. After applying the insulation, tape all the edges so there are no gaps, especially around the windows and doors.

Housewraps, or plastic sheeting used on the outside of a house before the siding is applied, are supposed to breathe and at the same time prevent wind from penetrating the building. We prefer standard, black 15 lb. tar paper, because it is less slippery and easier to put on. Housewrap is made from a material similar to courier envelopes, and it is supposed to be rip proof; however, we have found that after 10 or 15 years it can lose its strength and tear easily.

Roofing

Your choice of roofing material is determined by aesthetics, cost, climate and location. Most commonly used roofing materials include shingles, shakes, asphalt shingles and rolled roofing. Cedar shingles look terrific, but, of course, are more expensive and time-consuming to install.

Slope Run to Rise Ratio

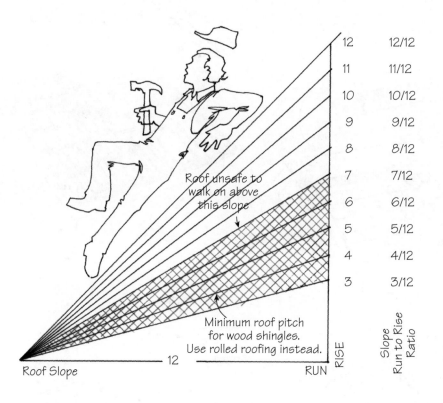

12	12/12
11	11/12
10	10/12
9	9/12
8	8/12
7	7/12
6	6/12
5	5/12
4	4/12
3	3/12

Roof unsafe to walk on above this slope

Minimum roof pitch for wood shingles. Use rolled roofing instead.

Roof Slope   12   RUN   RISE   Slope Run to Rise Ratio

Roofing Materials

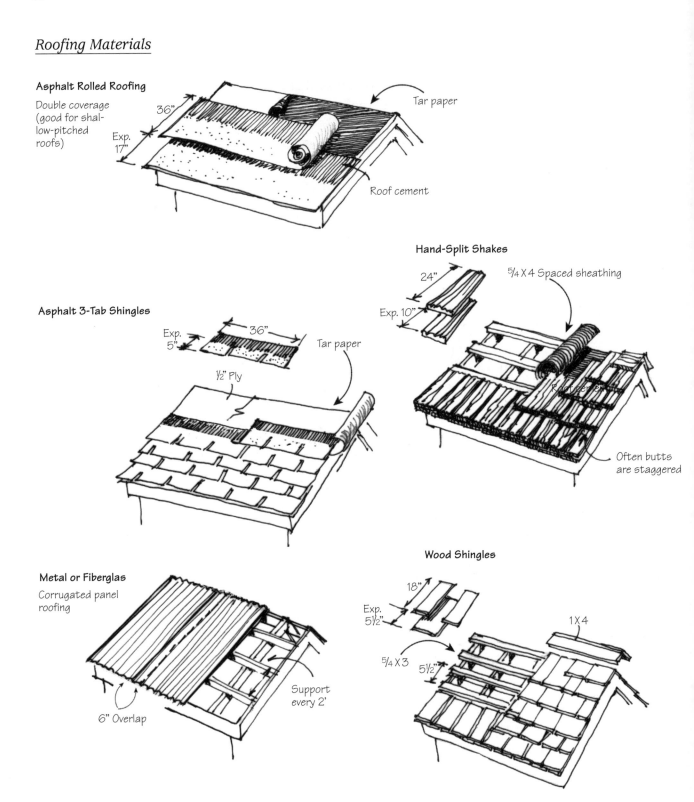

Asphalt Rolled Roofing

Double coverage (good for shallow-pitched roofs)

36"

Exp. 17"

Tar paper

Roof cement

Asphalt 3-Tab Shingles

Exp. 5"

36"

½" Ply

Tar paper

Hand-Split Shakes

24"

Exp. 10"

5/4 X 4 Spaced sheathing

Roof rafter

Often butts are staggered

Metal or Fiberglas

Corrugated panel roofing

6" Overlap

Support every 2'

Wood Shingles

18"

Exp. 5½"

5/4 X 3

5½"

1 X 4

Note: Exp. = Exposed Portion

Wood Shingling

The most common length for cedar shingles is 18", while hand-split shakes are generally 24". Shakes can vary in thickness and give a more rustic appearance to a roof. Eighteen inch shingles require an exposed portion of 5 1/2", whereas 24" hand-split shakes should have 10" exposed to the weather. Generally, a slope of 4" in a 12" rise is necessary for proper runoff of rainwater.

When shingling a roof, the first course is doubled—one layer on top of another—and the second course is laid so that no joints line up with the preceding joints. In conventional house construction, saturated felt, or tar paper, is used between the courses of hand-split shakes. The best base for wood shingles and shakes is 1x4 spruce sheathing. Space the boards 5 1/2" on center for shingles and 10" on center for hand-split shakes.

18" Cedar Shingles

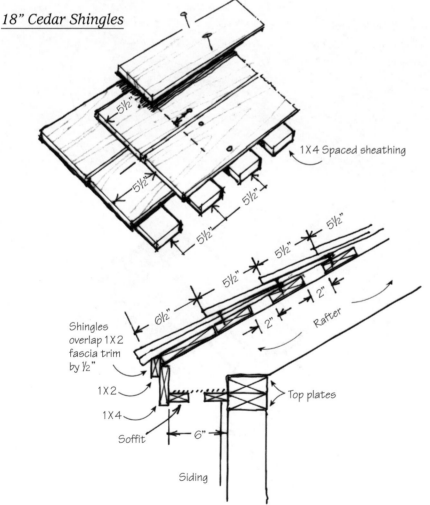

Roofing shingles are sold by the bundle and figured by the "square." which is 10'x10' or 100 square feet. It takes about four to five bundles of cedar shingles to cover a 10'x10' square and six to eight bundles of hand-split shakes to cover a square. Both shingles and shakes should overlap the eave by 1 1/4" and the sides by 1/2". Make sure that you nail on the fascia and the gable trim before you start shingling. Nail the gable trim directly to the ends of the 1x4 spaced sheathing. You can also nail shingles directly over plywood instead of spaced sheathing; however, only spaced sheathing allows ventilation for the shingles. In addition, 1x4 boards are easier to handle and take almost the same amount of time to nail as plywood. Spaced sheathing boards also create a natural holding rack for the shingles when you work on the roof.

24" Hand-Split Cedar Shakes

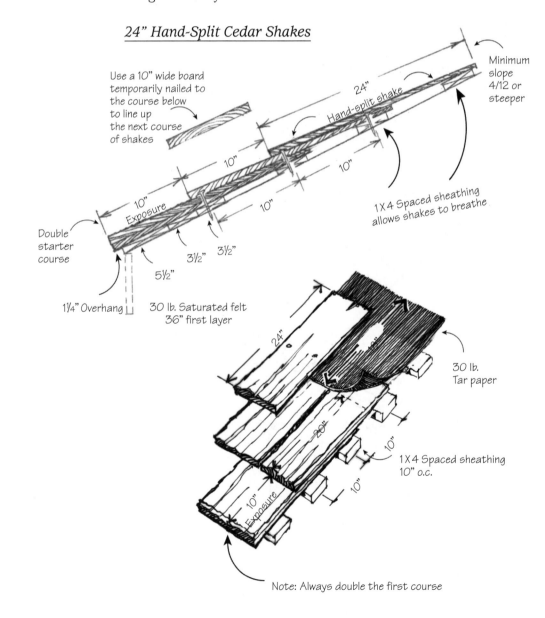

Note: Always double the first course

Asphalt roofing has improved in appearance over the last 20 years and comes in many colors. It is an inexpensive and less time-consuming alternative to cedar shingles and shakes, however, it is not as rustic looking. To start the roof, create a base for the first row of shingles by nailing on a starter course of shingles upside down with the tabs (slots) pointing toward the peak. Nail the starter shingles to the front edge of the roof, allowing a 3/8" overhang. Cover the starter shingles with a row of shingles, facing the tabs down. Nail four 3/8" head galvanized roofing nails, 5/8" above the slots of each shingle. Before starting the next row, cut the first shingle in half so that the cut-outs are staggered from row to row. Each row must be off-set by one-half a tab from the preceding row so that the slots do not line up (see illustration). Each row of shingles should be 5" above the preceding one. Snap a chalkline 5" above the lower edge of the last row installed, then line up the bottom edges of the next course of shingles along the chalk line. Once you have put on six or seven rows, measure from the ridge to see if the rows are even. If they are not even, adjust each remaining row slightly in order to finish evenly at the top.

Asphalt 3-Tab Shingles

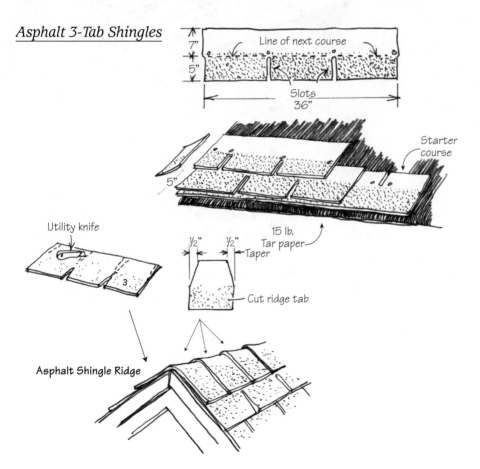

Roofing Tips

Tip: Use a 1X6 board as a straightedge to rest the butt end of each shingle.

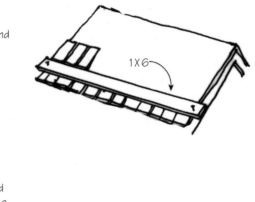

Tip: When nailing the 1X4 spaced sheathing onto the rafters, use a spacer made from scrap wood.

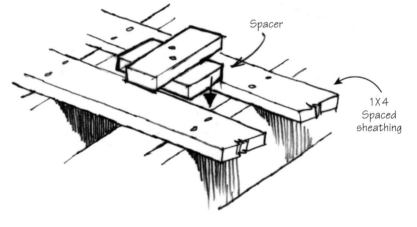

Electricity

While you are waiting for building and board of health permits to be approved, make arrangements for a temporary source of electric power so that you are ready to begin construction when all the permits and materials are available. If you are building in an area that does not have a nearby source of electricity, consider buying a generator to run your power tools. When your cabin is finished, you can use the generator to run a small refrigerator, water pump, compost toilet, electric lights, or even to charge a cell phone.

If you will only be using a power tool occasionally (two or three hours a day), you may only need a 3500 watt portable generator; however, if you need electricity to run several electrical appliances at once for an extended period of time, then you will need at least a 6000 watt generator.

Generators are rated in watts, not volts or amps. To compute how many watts you will need to run your equipment, look on the manufacturer's label of each tool or appliance. Our electric toaster, for example, uses 800 watts. Light bulbs are easy to figure out, since they are sold using watts to identify them. When figuring out the total wattage, use the "rated output," not the "maximum output," which indicates the short initial surge of power some appliances take. If you are still unsure of your wattage requirements, take a list of all your tools and appliances to your generator supplier, and ask them to recommend the appropriate generator. Remember, you will probably not be using all the tools and appliances at once.

Generators use regular gas or propane and require periodic oiling, sometimes as much as once a day. Some have a feature that automatically shuts off the generator when the oil gets too low, preventing it from overheating.

If you are using propane gas to heat your cabin or to cook with, you can also use it to operate your generator by installing a simple converter.

Store your generator away from your cabin and protect it from the elements. Even the best generators make an annoying noise, so try and situate it where there is some sort of sound barrier between the generator and your cabin. Old generators with their manual pulls can be hard to start, so you may want to spend some extra money on an electric start, to save your back.

If you know that you are going to be using electricity in your cabin, call your local electric power company and have them hook up a temporary electric meter panel on your property. If they run the line overhead, you may have to supply a temporary post. This should be a sturdy, 12' to 16' long 6x6 post, buried 3' into the ground near the building site, to support the meter panel box and the AC power outlet. Take into consideration that you may have concrete or other tall trucks making deliveries to your site, and make sure that the power line will not be in the way. Another option is to have the power line buried in the ground. This has many advantages but will be more expensive. Discuss your situation with the utility company and establish a firm price as to what the installation and monthly expenses will be. If you decide on an underground line, have the 2' to 4' deep trench dug with a backhoe at the same time as the foundation is being dug or the road is being built. You may be able to run a telephone or water line in the same trench, depending on your situation and local laws.

Bringing electricity to your cabin can be an expensive proposition depending on how far you are from the nearest utility pole. Some utility companies will supply you with one pole, approximately 200' in from the road, but you must pay for the remaining poles. In most cases, you will be responsible for cutting down trees to clear the path. Call your local utility company to find out what is required. Most cabins require a 200 amp service.

In a typical situation, three overhead wires (called a service drop) will be run from the nearest utility pole to the roof of your cabin. If the line crosses a driveway it must be a minimum of 12' high. The

Service Drop

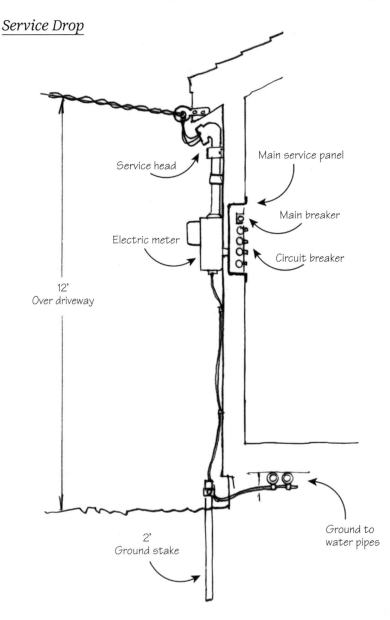

Service head

Main service panel

Main breaker

Electric meter

Circuit breaker

12'
Over driveway

2'
Ground stake

Ground to
water pipes

Electric wiring must be done before you install insulation; therefore it is a good idea to take photographs of each wall before insulating so, in the future, you will know exactly where the wires run.

wires will then run down a 2" diameter metal mast to an electric meter, through the wall of the cabin, to the panel box which houses the circuit breakers.

Although they are costly to run, electric baseboard heaters or wall heaters do provide quiet, dust-free heat. To avoid having to leave the heat on during long periods of cold weather when no one is in the cabin, it's a good idea to provide a simple way to drain the water pipes so that they won't freeze. You can easily accomplish this by opening a drain valve at the lowest level of your plumbing system. In very cold regions, make sure not to run the supply lines where they can freeze in cold weather, causing the pipes to burst and the cabin to flood once the spring thaw arrives. For the same reason, it's a good idea to turn off the circuit breaker that controls the water pump. This way, if your pipes do burst, only the few quarts of water left standing in the pipes will leak out.

Extension Cords

If you are forced to run a long, heavy-duty extension cord to your building site you run the risk of burning up the motors on power tools, since they are designed to run on a full load of electricity. The longer the cord, the greater the drain on electric current. Since this can ruin the tool and cause a fire, try to avoid it. Always use grounded three-pole extension cords.

Extension cords seem to have a mind of their own when it comes to coiling them up after use. The key is to coil them up from the same end each time (for instance, from the power source end). The best way we have found to keep them coiled is to cut a 1 1/2" wide section of automobile inner tube and loop it around the coil. The friction from the rubber strap keeps the coil wrapped tight.

Water

Divining (Dowsing)
for Water Source

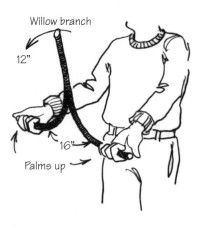

Willow branch

12"

16"

Palms up

In remote areas where there are no streams or lakes nearby, fresh water must be carried to a cabin. This chore can be minimized by having a way of collecting rainwater. If you only need to collect water for washing and not for drinking, you can simply put a rain barrel under the roof gutter. If your goal is to collect a substantial amount of water, a cistern is required. If your cabin roof measures 16'x20', or 320 square feet, and the average rainfall is 3" per month, then you could collect 480 gallons of water per month.

If you are lucky enough to have a cabin site near a spring or stream that is located uphill from your cabin, you can tap into the water source by running a pipe from the stream to your cabin, and let gravity deliver the water to you. The higher the stream, the better the water pressure. Since the pipe is generally exposed, this is a good method to use in warm climates where there is no chance that the pipes will freeze. Take into consideration, however, that a hot summer can dry up a stream, leaving you with no fresh water.

If your cabin is situated above a lake, you can use a pump to pipe water up to the cabin. Our friends in Maine pump their water from the lake through PCB hose to iron pipes and store it in a large zinc tank in their attic. The tank is cleaned each spring and kept covered with netting during the summer. The pump is powered by a gasoline motor with a pull-start, like an outboard, and a hose can be attached for fire protection. Remember that fresh water will freeze in the winter, so make sure to provide easily accessible water turn-off valves to allow the water to drain. Even if you think your water is potable, have it checked yearly by the local health department. If in doubt, boil the water for 20 minutes and add a pinch of salt to improve the taste. Halazone tablets, bought at camping supply stores, can also be used to purify the water.

Finding Water

A drilled or driven well, bringing up water from underground, is the most convenient way to bring water into your cabin. The water, hopefully, is safe from contamination and surface pollutants, and the water does not freeze since it comes from below the frost level. Water is generally found below layers of sand, gravel, porous rock or cracks in the rock. Sand is the easiest material to drill through and gives you the best tasting water.

Some people swear by diviners, who walk your property, holding a forked willow stick. When it points down toward the ground, it is supposed to indicate a good spot to drill for water. It is said that Frank Lloyd Wright dramatically planted his walking stick in the ground and announced, "You will find water here!" and they did. We paid a dowser $300 to walk our property, using a magnometer, and advise us where to drill. We finally hit water 350' through solid rock and $3000 later!

Instead of pounding a pipe into the ground and hoping you might not hit bedrock, you might consider buying or renting a portable gas-powered rotary drill and drilling the well yourself. The rotary drill consists of either a rock cutting bit or an earth cutting bit, screwed to a 5' length of hollow stem pipe. Water is pumped down the stem pipe while the bit is turning, and the debris or cuttings from the hole are forced up the outside of the pipe to the surface of the ground, where they flow into two ditches—one for removing the debris and the other for recycling the water back down the pipe into the hole. Ironically, it takes water to drill for water, so you must have at least a 500 gallon drum of water to start drilling, plus a 3 HP water pump to move it. You can pump water up from a nearby lake or stream, or, if you have road access to the cabin, you can truck in large tanks of water.

Once you reach the water table, you can pull up the pipe using a winch, mounted on a rig, and exchange the bit for a 5' length of perforated pipe which screens out the sandlike particles. Then the 5' sections of plastic well casing pipe are stacked and glued on top of the well screen or strainer pipe, to prevent contamination. The sides are packed with pea gravel to invite the transmission of ground water to the screen and to hold the casing in place. The top 15' to 20' are sealed with clay or cement to keep out ground water. Once the well is in place, it is cleaned by forcing out any remaining particles using water pressure from the pump.

To bring up water from the well, you can use a cast iron hand pump attached to the well stem pipe with a coupling. Since the temperature, 10' below the surface of the ground remains constant, the well water is protected from frost. On very cold days, you might have to pour boiling water into the pump in order to get it going. However, unlike other well water systems that rely on electric pumps that can fail during emergencies, you will always have water. We once restored a house, built in 1804, for a client who had a pump outside her kitchen door. Every time there was an electrical outage, her neighbors would come to her house, buckets in hand, to get fresh water.

Do-It-Yourself Well Drilling

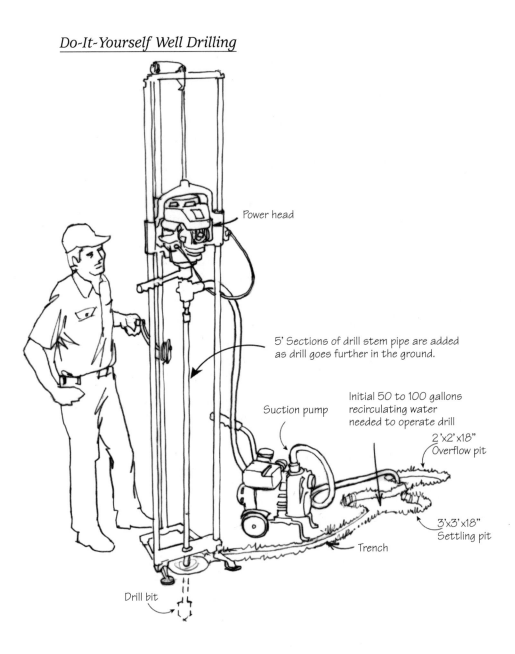

Power head

5' Sections of drill stem pipe are added as drill goes further in the ground.

Suction pump

Initial 50 to 100 gallons recirculating water needed to operate drill

2'x2'x18" Overflow pit

3'x3'x18" Settling pit

Trench

Drill bit

If you have electricity supplied to your cabin, or if you have a gas powered water pump that you can start and run for a few minutes each day, you can store enough water in a holding tank to last several days. To find out how big a tank you need, estimate that two people use a minimum of 125 gallons per day. This includes 50 gallons for toilet flushing, 40 gallons for bathing, and approximately 5 gallons for washing dishes. If you have a privy, you will only need a reservoir of 75 gallons, which would fit nicely into an 80 gallon tank.

Plumbing and Sanitary Systems

Plumbing can be an expensive part of building, even if you are only fitting pipes for a small cabin. If you are a do-it-yourself type, you might try installing some of the plumbing yourself, such as the final hook-up to your fixtures. Leave the rough plumbing to professionals, to make sure that it is vented and installed properly and that there are no health hazards or contamination.

Check to see if your cabin is situated in an area where building codes or board of health regulations allow PVC plumbing for water supply lines, and whether or not it is limited to cold water pipes and drain pipes. Since these plastic pipes and fittings came on the market, plumbing installation has become much easier for the average homeowner and do-it-yourselfer. PVC plastic pipes can be installed in far less time and much more easily than their iron or copper counterparts. For example, running a pipe to the other side of your cabin and installing an outside tap might run you $150 if a plumber does it, while you can do it in less than an hour for $20 worth of materials. You will need a fine-tooth saw (such as a hack saw), some PVC cement and a tape measure. PVC pipe comes in 10' lengths, is generally 1/2" inside diameter, and can be joined to another PVC pipe with a simple coupling. All you need to do is measure the length of pipe you need, cut it with a saw, and glue the pieces together. The nice thing about PVC pipe is that since it is flexible, measurements don't have to be as precise as with iron or brass pipe. If you cut a piece of tubing too short, you can easily afford to discard it and start over.

Materials

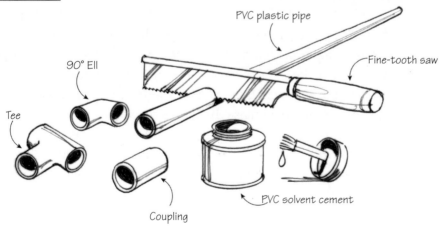

PVC plastic pipe

Fine-tooth saw

90° Ell

Tee

Coupling

PVC solvent cement

PVC pipe costs only about one-fifth the cost of copper pipe. A friend of ours lived for several years in a log cabin in a rural part of West Virginia. His wife got tired of bathing in a stream, bought herself some plumbing supplies and PVC pipe and installed indoor plumbing in less than a week. No more hauling water from the stream. Just like electrical wiring, plumbing should be done while the framing is exposed.

Plumbing can be installed under your cabin if it is carefully insulated. Provide a removable access panel to the crawl space under the cabin, in case any plumbing has to be repaired. Insulating the interior foundation walls in the crawl space with 2" of rigid Styrofoam not only helps keep any exposed pipes from freezing, but also makes the floor less chilly. A little antifreeze should be poured into the toilet, sink and tub traps to keep them from freezing when you are gone.

Sanitary Systems

The sanitary system that you choose depends a great deal on how often you plan to use your cabin. If you visit your cabin only sporadically, you may not feel you need indoor plumbing at all.

If your cabin is far from an electric power supply or running water and you want a more permanent sanitary system, you may want to consider one of the composting toilets. These self-contained units require no water or external plumbing—only a 3" plastic vent pipe, and they will not freeze up in winter. Through aeration, evaporation and microbe activity, almost 90 per cent of the waste in the bottom compartment of the toilet decomposes, leaving a compost that can be recycled into your flower garden when mixed with peat moss. The decomposition is made possible by a wind driven turbine, mounted on top of a vent stack forcing fresh air down to aerate the waste matter in the toilet. Occasionally, the mixture has to be raked by hand and/or removed to a compost pile. It uses a chemical additive and peat moss to increase the rate of decomposition and manufacturers claim that it is odorless. This system is not cheap, but the idea that you are recycling something that could be potentially harmful into something safe and useful makes it worth the expense for many people.

Outhouses

A landmark of rural North America is the backyard outhouse. It has long been the butt of humor and practical jokes, and has become almost extinct as urban sprawl invades the countryside. Most suburban communities have outlawed them because of the possibility that they could pollute water supplies. However, if your cabin is in a remote area, inaccessible to the general public and not regulated by building and health regulations, and if you are willing to clean and maintain a working outhouse that does not jeopardize your water supply, this may be the best solution. Make sure, however, to check for any local health restrictions and building codes before expending your time and energy.

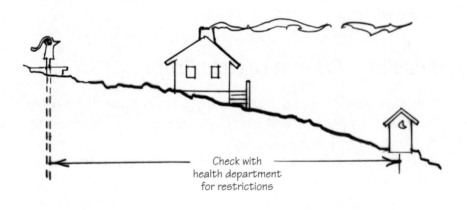

Check with
health department
for restrictions

If your property is regulated by the local building department's board of health, of if you wish to include sewage from your kitchen sink and bath in your disposal system, then you will need a septic tank and absorption field. This is a masonry tank buried near the cabin. The overflow is fed by gravity through a pipe into a series of parallel trenches in an absorption field. The soil in the field must be tested to see if it percolates sufficiently to meet the board of health

Typical Septic System

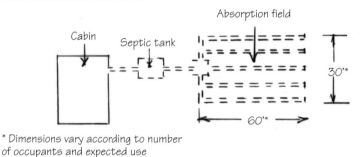

* Dimensions vary according to number
of occupants and expected use

requirements. This requires a licensed engineer or an architect and a mason to build the septic, plumb the cabin tank and lay the lines. The absorption field is sized according to the amount of people expected to use the sanitary system on any given day, so it may be as large as 30'x60'.

Leaching Pit and Grease Traps

This is an essential part of planning any cabin and one that must be dealt with in a practical and ecological manner, while disturbing the environment as little as possible.

Unless you hire a contractor to install a board of health approved septic system, you must have a way of disposing of grey water. You will need to build a leaching pit and, if your shower and sink are heavily used, a grease trap and absorption area. The size of the pit and field are determined by the number of people using the water and the expected frequency of use. The local building department can provide you with information. To give you a rough idea of the required dimensions, a leaching pit that serves two or three people who use their cabin only ten weekends a year, would be roughly three concrete blocks high and three and one-half blocks wide. These blocks are laid up dry inside a hole, dug 36" deep and 5' wide, allowing space for 6" of 1" to 2" diameter stones, placed under and around the blocks. The blocks are covered with 2" concrete slabs, sold at most masonry supply outlets, and 6" of dirt. In theory, all the grey water from sinks and tubs comes through a 3" diameter PVC pipe, 2" from the top of the pit and falls to the rocks below where it is filtered through the undisturbed soil.

Leaching Pits and Grease Traps for Grey Water

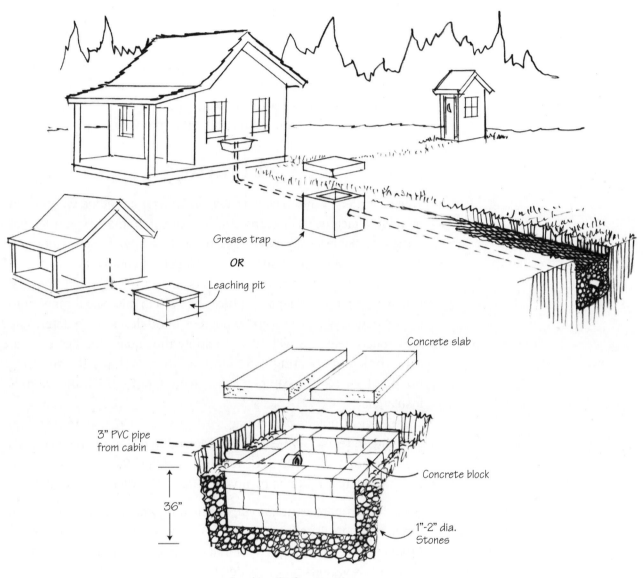

Grease trap

OR

Leaching pit

Concrete slab

3" PVC pipe from cabin

36"

Concrete block

1"-2" dia. Stones

Leaching Pit Construction

No matter what type of septic system you use, make sure to draw a plan, using cross references, indicating where it is buried and file it in a safe place.

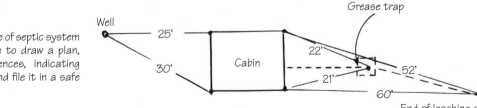

Well

Grease trap

25'

22'

Cabin

30'

21'

52'

60'

End of leaching area

Map of Well & Septic System

If you live in a cabin with several people all summer, this may not be sufficient. A more advanced system is to have a grease trap that skims off the semi-solid soap grease and scum. The grey water then passes into an absorption field and is filtered into the ground. Similar to the leaching pit, the grease trap can be built out of concrete blocks, but instead of being porous, it is water tight and has to be pumped out after a few years of use. Always check with your local board of health to find out what is required in your area.

Heating

There are many ways to heat a cabin and the right method will depend on a lot of factors, such as the size of your cabin, the type of fuel that is most available locally (wood, gas, oil or electricity), the insulation you have used in your cabin and how cold it gets in your area.

Heating requirements are calculated in BTU (British Thermal Units), which is the quantity of heat required to raise the temperature of one pound of water from 59 degrees to 60 degrees. To determine how much heat you will need, multiply the square footage of your cabin times the heating zone number, then multiply the resulting number by 1.5 if the cabin is not insulated, or by 0.7 if the cabin is insulated.

For example, a cabin that is 12'x16' has 192 square feet, and 192 square feet x 50 (heating zone for middle United States) equals a base amount of 9,600 BTUs required. Multiply 9,600 x 1.5 (if cabin is not insulated) and this means 14,400 BTUs will be required.

To compare various types of heating appliances, look for the manufacturer's list of specifications to see how many BTUs each one produces. The following is a list that can give you a rough idea of how many BTUs various products deliver.

Candle	2,000 BTU
Kerosene lamp	2,000 BTU
Propane catalytic heater	3,000 BTU
Electric space heater	5,122 BTU
Radiant infra-red propane heater	6,000-15,000 BTU
Kerosene space heater	23,000 BTU
Vented gas heater	40,000 BTU
Large potbelly wood-burning stove	13,500 BTU
Boxwood wood-burning stove	15,000 BTU
Franklin wood-burning stove	12,000 BTU
Hearthstone wood-burning stove	50,000 BTU

The efficiency of the wood-burning stove can be improved by resting an Ecofan on top of the stove. This is operated by heat energy converted into electricity that in turn operates a small fan that blows hot air throughout the room. Using wood to heat your cabin should not be a problem if you are using the cabin for occasional weekends, but you should consider an electric, oil or gas furnace if you intend to use your cabin all winter.

Electric Heaters

Safety tips to keep in mind when using electric heaters:
- Don't use extension cords with your heater.
- Don't dry clothes over a space heater.
- Never leave your cabin with a heater running.
- Unless your heater is a wall-mounted model, make sure that it has tip-over protection.
- Only use a heater that has been tested at an independent lab, such as UL or ETL.
- Never use a heater that has corroded metal or melted plastic casing, a cord with frayed wires or bent plug blades.

Propane Gas

Propane tanks have a label that indicates the "tare weight" or TW number, which is the weight of the tank when it is full. If you are wondering how much gas is left in the tank, use your bathroom scales to weigh the tank and subtract this weight from the full tank weight.

Tank Capacity	Tank Weight
4 1/2 gallons	40 pounds when full
23 gallons	100 pounds when full
47 gallons	200 pounds when full
100 gallons	420 pounds when full

Note: With the exception of electric heaters, all combustible fossil fuel heaters give off varying amounts of harmful carbon monoxide. To play it safe, install a carbon monoxide detector in your cabin, and always provide a permanent opening or vent to bring fresh air into your cabin, even if it means losing a little of your precious warm air. People have died, asleep in air-tight enclosures such as campers, as a result of lack of oxygen. Small, screened, non-operable louvers are sold at the lumber yard, and attractive teak vents can be bought at most marine supply stores.

Wood-Burning Stoves

Cast iron wood-burning stoves became popular in the 1970s and 80s and in many cases replaced wood-burning fireplaces because of their efficiency. Not only do they heat your cabin, but they can also be used to cook dinner. They range in price from the Boxwood heat stove to the huge, old camp stoves, like the Atlantic Queen or Elmira. All you need is a good supply of firewood. As with anything that burns, precautions should be taken when using these stoves, as they can get red hot when stoked too much. For cabin dwellers who want to see an open flame, there is always the Franklin stove that has doors that can be left open. This type of stove works on both convection and radiation principles of heating and are 40 to 50 per cent efficient.

Almost all wood-burning stoves require a 6" diameter sheet metal stove pipe with a damper to control the rate of combustion. If you plan to use your stove often, you should buy insulated stove pipe, which consists of two stove pipes (one inside the other), with a 1" air space between them. A thimble is also necessary where the stove pipe goes through the roof. Allow a 2" space between the stove pipe and any combustible roofing materials. A flanged base is used above the roof and acts as flashing to keep the rainwater out. The top of the stove pipe should be 2' above any point that is 10' from the sloping roof. If the stove pipe is too high, you will have to secure it to the roof, using thin wires or roof braces. To prevent squirrels from getting into the cabin, place a cap over the top of the stove pipe. This also helps keep the rain out.

Stove Installation

The stove should stand on a concrete or brick base and should be raised 6" off the floor. Especially if children will be in the cabin, put a three-panel metal screen in front of the stove to keep them from touching the hot metal. Keep a fire extinguisher near the stove door or a 5 gallon plastic jug filled with water. If your cabin is left unheated in cold climates, put some antifreeze in with the water (marked "poison") to keep it from freezing. Put fires out before leaving your cabin, even if you will only be gone a short time.

Heating: Wood-Burning Stoves

Boxwood

Railroad potbelly
stove

1. Convection heat is used in forced hot air systems all over the country. The air is heated up in a furnace, blown by a fan and transported to the areas in which it is needed, circulating throughout the room.

2. Conduction heat is used in wood-burning cast iron stoves. The heat is conducted through the metal walls and warms the air around it.

3. Radiant heat, as from a fireplace, throws off heat rays and can be felt some distance away from the heat source.

Cook Stove
Atlantic Queen

Folding Door
Franklin Stove

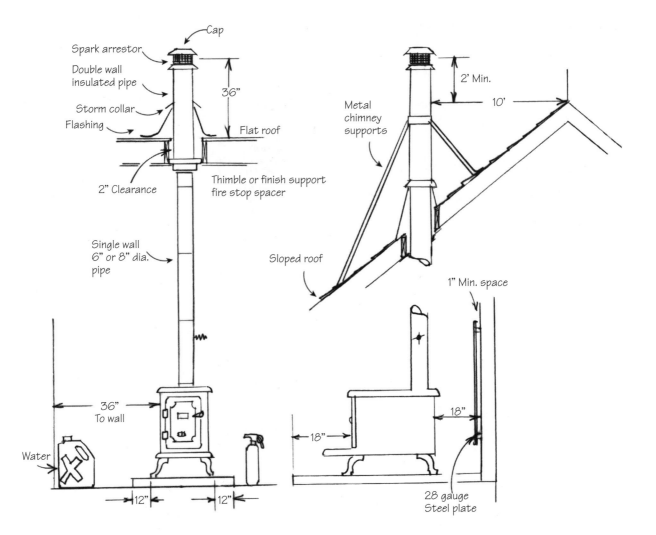

Cap

Spark arrestor

Double wall
insulated pipe

Storm collar

Flashing

36"

Flat roof

2" Clearance

Thimble or finish support
fire stop spacer

Single wall
6" or 8" dia.
pipe

36"
To wall

Water

12"   12"

Metal
chimney
supports

2' Min.

10'

Sloped roof

1" Min. space

18"

18"

28 gauge
Steel plate

Needless to say, wood-burning stoves can get extremely hot when filled to capacity, so situate the stove at least 18" away from the back wall and install a 28 gauge sheet of steel behind it. Mount the steel plate so that it stands 1" away from the wall to allow air to circulate behind it. Otherwise, place the stove at least 36" away from the wall. Don't forget that the stove pipe also gets hot, especially just above the top of the stove. The pipe also radiates a lot of heat into the cabin.

When choosing a wood-burning stove, there are several things to consider. One of the least obvious is how you are going to transport it to your cabin. If your cabin is at the end of an easily accessible road, there is no problem. However, if the stove weighs 200 pounds and has to be transported through the woods, make sure you have a vehicle that can carry it and an access road that is suitable for your vehicle.

Another consideration is how long the stove will hold heat. This will become apparent the first cold night you spend in your cabin by how many times you have to get up during the night to add fuel and stoke the fire. Generally speaking, the greater the mass (of steel or iron), plus how air tight and well made the stove is, determines how long the stove retains its heat. One way to help keep a fire going longer is to minimize its air supply by adjusting the damper.

Fireplaces

For those of us who relish the look and feel of a traditional stone or brick fireplace, the loss of efficiency (10 to 15 per cent) is compensated for by the satisfaction we feel watching the flames sparkle and the embers glow. Human beings have stared into fires for thousands of years to warm their bodies and lift their spirits.

A good way to construct a working fireplace is to buy a manufactured steel plate liner, such as a Heatilater, and to build the masonry around it. By doing this, you avoid having to worry about critical firebox measurements, smoke shelves or dampers, since they are built into the Heatilater. If you are building with stone, as we did, make sure you have two to three times more stone than you need, since you will have to be very selective in fitting the stones together. We used a homemade yoke to haul smooth stones up from the beach, but you might want to simply go to a masonry supply yard, hand pick the stones that you like and have them delivered.

When you are picking out stones, keep an eye out for one that can serve as your keystone for the center of the arch above the fireplace. The keystone is the last stone placed in an arch. Because of its shape, it exerts diagonal pressure on the stones on either side of it, locking the arch in place. We have seen arches in Turkey built without mortar, more than 2,000 years old, that are still standing, using this principle. When building your fireplace, position the stones directly above the firebox opening in a slight curve, temporarily resting them on a curved piece of wood, and removing the wood when you are finished. Early Roman building laws required that architects of any arch must stand under it while the falsework was removed, so that he would be the first to know if anything had gone wrong!

Fireplace Construction

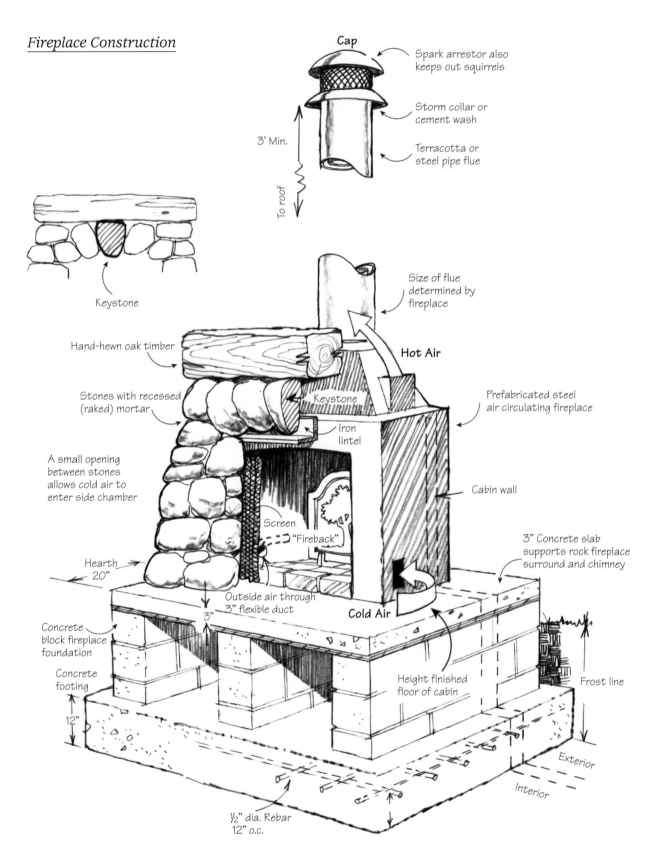

Cap

Spark arrestor also keeps out squirrels

Storm collar or cement wash

Terracotta or steel pipe flue

3' Min.

To roof

Keystone

Size of flue determined by fireplace

Hand-hewn oak timber

Hot Air

Stones with recessed (raked) mortar

Keystone

Prefabricated steel air circulating fireplace

Iron lintel

A small opening between stones allows cold air to enter side chamber

Cabin wall

Screen

"Fireback"

3" Concrete slab supports rock fireplace surround and chimney

Hearth 20"

Outside air through 3" flexible duct

Cold Air

3"

Concrete block fireplace foundation

Height finished floor of cabin

Concrete footing

Frost line

12"

Exterior

Interior

½" dia. Rebar 12" o.c.

Make sure you have a hefty foundation under the fireplace to carry the weight of the fireplace and chimney and extend the masonry hearth at least 20" from the fireplace. This not only complies with code, but it also helps prevent sparks from landing on a wooden floor. To be extra safe, tile the floor 5' out in front of the fireplace and always use a spark screen in front of an open fire.

Most metal fireplace liners have a heat circulating feature which draws cool air off the floor. The air passes up two side chambers where it is heated through the side walls of the fireplace and exits out two openings at the top. A heavy oak timber often serves as a mantel and should be 8" to 12" above the fireplace opening so that the wood won't catch on fire. To support the stone facing at the top, buy a piece of 3"x3" angle-iron from your local masonry supplier to use as a lintel.

Positioning a cast iron "fireback" against the back wall of the fireplace serves two purposes: it helps protect the back wall and it radiates heat forward.

Firewood

To feed a wood stove or a fireplace, you will need a lot of seasoned firewood, which you can either buy or cut and split yourself. When buying cordwood, be aware that a full cord measures 4'x4'x8', while a face cord measures only 4'x8' by the length of each fireplace-sized log. Before you agree on a price, make sure to discuss where the wood will be delivered, and try to get them to stack it near the cabin rather than dumping it in a pile at the end of the road. If possible, build a covered shed to hold your firewood.

Keep in mind that when you are trying to heat a weekend cabin that has been unheated for several days, the cabin must be tempered before it will feel really warm. Remember, every square inch of wall surface has behind it a mass of cold material that has to be warmed up before the walls, ceiling and floor feel warm. This can take several days.

Carrying firewood from the wood shed into your cabin on a rainy, cold night can put a damper on your evening. One good solution is to provide a firewood access door and storage bin next to the fireplace. This insulated, hinged door is unlocked from the inside and allows you to replenish your firewood supply without making a mess on the floor.

CUTTING AND BURNING FIREWOOD

Firewood Shed

- Make sure that you are burning seasoned logs. Heavy wood is usually "green" wood and can be difficult to burn. A few pieces of "green" wood can be used as backlogs and will burn more slowly, but use more than a few pieces and you will have a cold cabin.

- Split logs in the winter, if possible, as the frozen sap in the wood makes logs easier to split.

- Since the hard part of splitting logs is bending over, try propping up two or three logs in an old car tire and then whack away with your splitting maul while you walk around the tire.

- Use a maul, not a cutting ax, to split logs. Protect the neck of the maul with rubber tape or get a Fiberglas handle.

- If the log doesn't split after one or two tries, use a wedge and the back of a maul to split it open. Once a log is split halfway open, you can generally split the rest without using the wedge.

- Always work in a cleared flat area with no overhanging limbs.

- If the wood is unseasoned, stack it in a "crib" shape to allow the maximum amount of air to circulate around each log. Once the wood is seasoned, stack logs with the bark side up.
- Don't clean out the ashes after every fire. There should be a bank of ashes in the back of the firebox to help reflect the heat and to protect the back of the fireplace from excessive heat.
- To help prevent smoke from entering the cabin rather than the chimney, when you are first starting a fire carefully hold a burning torch of newspaper up the open flue. This helps direct the warm air up the chimney.
- Build your fire using paper, twigs, light kindling, smaller logs and heavier logs, in that order.
- Never try to make a fire with less than three logs. Use andirons or arrange the logs so there is a slight gap between them, enabling oxygen to feed the fire.
- Red oak is hard to burn; white oak is easy.
- Cedar and spruce cause sparks.
- Don't leave a fire unattended without closing the fire screen. Put out fires when leaving the cabin.
- If you are cutting your own trees for firewood, make sure to cut logs the correct length and to make perpendicular cuts so the logs will stand up straight on the ground when it comes time to split them.

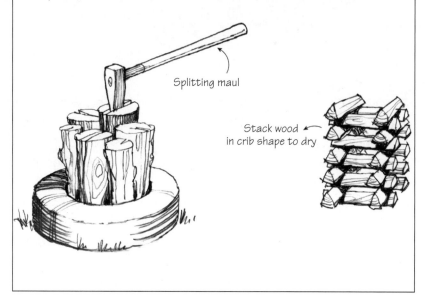

Splitting maul

Stack wood
in crib shape to dry

Cabin Reflections

Growing up in the midwest, Jeanie remembers visiting her closest friend, Amy Buckingham, whose family had a cluster of cabins overlooking Reams lake in Dent, Minnesota. As siblings grew and children were born, cabins were expanded to accommodate larger families. Screened-in porches were added and became cool sleeping areas for the kids—the best place to listen to crickets and whisper into the night. Although each family had their own cabin, they shared one campfire in the evening. It was the magnet that attracted all the different family members, the neutral ground, a place to gather and warm up during those wonderful, chilly Minnesota nights, and to hear about each other's days, roast marshmallows and eat s'mores. There was never an argument or sibling rivalry while sitting around the campfire. It created a closeness that did not exist while visiting another cabin.

Foster MacEdward, beter known as MacEagle, built his Vermont cabin (named "Eagle's Nest") in 1972. The view is spectacular, the cabin perched atop a mountain at the end of a steep one mile long road, surrounded by the Green Mountain National Forest. His neighbors include bear, moose, deer, and several species of birds. He still prefers to have no electricity, using the stars, moon and a few candles for a night light. Outdoor cooking is often done over a campfire made from smooth river stones. Inside a ladder reaches a loft, which sleeps twelve or more. This cabin was a favorite weekend retreat for Mac's two teenage daughters to bring friends, where they would bake braided bread over the campfire.

LOG CABINS

Our cabin is a magical retreat just 20 minutes from our year-round house. It's at the end of a barely passable road: then you descend 70 steps down a steep boulder and mountain laurel-strewn hillside. It is utterly simple and basic, not just in construction, but in spirit. It is free of the piles of the stuff-of-life that endlessly accumulate on surfaces and in corners of our home. There is nothing to do at the cabin but relax...

—Nancy Fitzpatrick, owner of The Red Lion

Building With Logs

Log cabins, an American tradition, were originally built by the pioneers, since there were plenty of trees available in the virgin forests of North America. In fact, the fewer than two dozen men making up the Lewis and Clark expedition in 1813 built a small log fort in three weeks. One of the advantages of building with logs is their thermal mass heat retention, which makes them an excellent insulator against the cold weather.

To join logs together at the ends, most log cabin builders used an "A-V" notch since it could be easily cut with an ax. After the introduction of the chain saw in the 1950s, many builders switched to the saddle notch. The chain saw enabled builders to use joining techniques that otherwise would have been too difficult and time-consuming.

Building a log cabin may require new skills with an ax or chain saw that the typical do-it-yourself builder does not have. Although you may spend less money on materials for a log cabin than you would spend using other building materials, you will definitely spend more time in the construction.

To give you a realistic idea of how much time it may take to build a log cabin, we contacted Don Gesinger, an architect in British Columbia, who started out building his own hexagonal-shaped log cabin northwest of Lake Winnipeg some 20 years ago. Since then, Don has become an expert in his field, having designed and built some of the largest and most beautiful log cabins in the province.

Before you decide to build a log cabin, test yourself on how much time it takes to cut a tree down, transport it, peel the bark off and cut the notches. Even a small cabin may require as many as 60 or more logs. Multiple that time by five hours per log. Add to this the time it takes to build the foundation, install the floors, walls, windows, doors and roofing, and you can begin to understand the time commitment required to build your dream. In spite of this lengthy process, people we have talked to who have built their own log cabins have no regrets and are justifiably proud of their efforts.

Time spent per log	Work to be performed
15 - 30 mins.	1. Walk through woods and find suitable logs.
30 - 60 mins.	2. Cut down tree and remove limbs.
30 - 60 mins.	3. Transport tree to building site.
10 mins.	4. Cut tree to final length.
60 mins. plus	5. Peel bark from tree.
60 mins.	6. Move log into place, mark and notch.
60 mins.	7. Test fit log and remove bumps so log fit.
15 - 30 mins.	8. Insert seal between logs.
15 - 30 mins.	9. Move log into place and spike with nails.
total	Approximately 5 - 7 hours

Note: This list will, of course, vary according to the size and type of trees available.

One thing to remember is that logs shrink as they age (which takes approximately three years). This should be taken into consideration when building the walls, windows and doors. A typical cabin using unseasoned logs may shrink in height as much as 6" over a period of years. One way to minimize this problem is to cut, peel and store the logs under a dry cover until they have a moisture content of less than 15 per cent. (See the Two-Bedroom Log Cabin later in this chapter, which shows a detail of how to compensate for this shrinkage in cabin height.)

Log Joints

Chinkless Joint

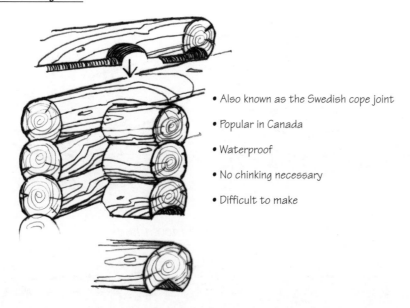

- Also known as the Swedish cope joint
- Popular in Canada
- Waterproof
- No chinking necessary
- Difficult to make

Perhaps the best, but most difficult to make, log joint is the chinkless, Swedish cope method. Each log is carved out on the bottom, using a scooped adze, to fit the irregularities of the log beneath it. The advantage of this joint is that rainwater is shed off the round sloped surface of the log below. In addition, the two longitudinal edges that contact this underlying log compress under the weight of the logs above, forming a tight seal.

A-V Joint   ## *Saddle Notch*

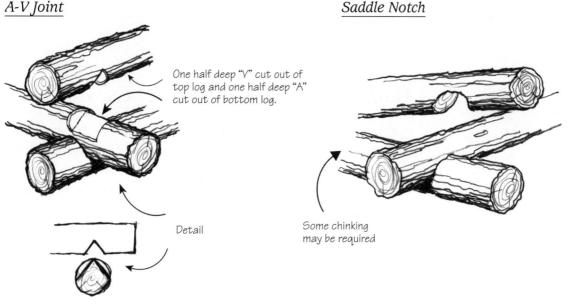

One half deep "V" cut out of top log and one half deep "A" cut out of bottom log.

Detail

Some chinking may be required

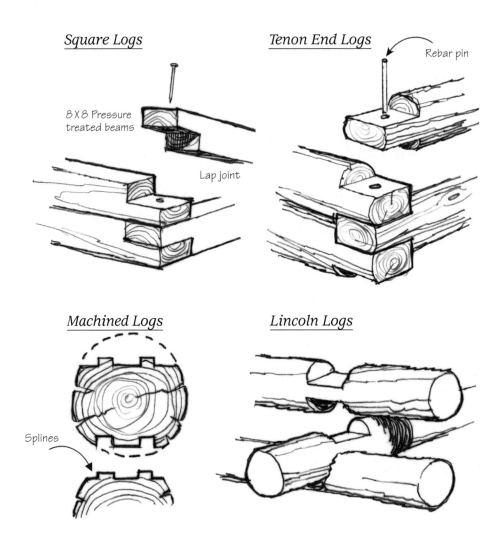

Square Logs

8 X 8 Pressure treated beams

Lap joint

Tenon End Logs

Rebar pin

Machined Logs

Splines

Lincoln Logs

Maine Woods Log Construction

In this type of construction the log ends do not extend past each other and therefore do not require the labor intensive notching. Instead, the log ends are cut off perpendicular to the length of the log and joined at the corners using what amounts to vertical posts which can be built in several ways, as shown on the next page. True, this sacrifices the traditional log cabin look, but the savings in labor are substantial. Care must be taken, however, to allow the logs to settle.

Maine Woods Style Log Construction

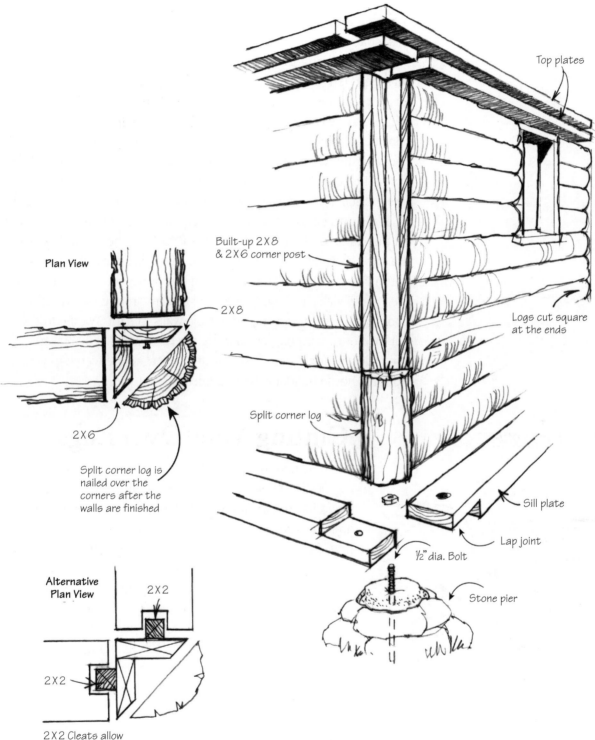

Top plates

Built-up 2 X 8
& 2 X 6 corner post

Logs cut square
at the ends

Split corner log

Sill plate

Lap joint

½" dia. Bolt

Stone pier

Plan View

2 X 8

2 X 6

Split corner log is
nailed over the
corners after the
walls are finished

**Alternative
Plan View**

2 X 2

2 X 2

2 X 2 Cleats allow
logs to settle

Milled Logs

If trudging through the woods, cutting down suitable trees, lugging them back to your site and peeling them does not strike your fancy, consider ordering the logs from a saw mill where they can cut, or mill them lengthwise, into consistent sized logs. This can save you a lot of construction time since you don't have to worry about the bumps, curves and natural tapering that exists in most trees. Logs of consistent shape are easier to seal together, and the connections between the windows, doors, roof and foundation are easier to make.

The saw mill can cut the logs into several profiles to create different effects. The most popular one is the "D" shaped log which has a flat top and bottom and a flat interior face, making the wall smooth on the inside of the cabin. If you want to keep the round log look on the interior as well, you can have the saw mill cut off just the top and bottom of each log. If you are having this done, you may want to save the cut-off slabs, as they can be used as trim around the windows and doors or as vertical siding on the gable walls (see the Two-Bedroom Log Cabin later in this chapter). If there are no saw mills in your area, you can order the logs cut to your specifications and delivered to your site from log home builders. (See Sources.)

"D" Log Profile

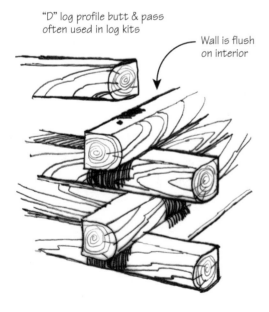

"D" log profile butt & pass
often used in log kits

Wall is flush
on interior

Cutting Your Own Logs

Begin by figuring out how many logs you will need and making a list of where each log will go. If you don't own your own wood lot, try writing to the Department of Forestry in your area and requesting a permit to harvest a specific number of trees from government land. Or, perhaps you have a friend or neighbor who wouldn't mind letting you cull 60 or more trees in return for permission to use your cabin occasionally. Impress upon all concerned that you will be very discriminating in your selection of trees, making sure not to take any that are less than 20' apart. In a dense forest, thinning the trees can actually be beneficial to the woods as a whole.

Choose your trees by holding up a straightedge or yardstick and checking them from all angles. The straighter the tree, the less headaches you will have later on. Mark each tree with bright surveyor's tape, writing what the log will be used for on the tape with a waterproof pen.

There are different opinions on the best time to fell trees. By cutting trees in the fall or winter, you have the advantage of skidding the logs over snow covered ground. However, felling the trees in the spring, when the sap is running, allows you to peel the wood more easily.

Before you start out, make sure that you have a 5 gallon can of gasoline, pre-mixed with the proper ratio of oil, and a wrench to adjust your chain saw. Most chain saws start to loosen after they warm up. Don't use a chain saw that is too big; the extra weight and vibration will quickly wear you out. A 16" to 18" cutting bar is sufficiently long. Wear a hard hat to protect yourself from falling dead branches and ear plugs to protect your ears. Goggles are also a good idea, to protect your eyes from branches, woodchips or branches snapping back in your face. Follow the cutting procedures as shown here and clear the ground around the tree so you can make a fast exit when the tree begins to fall.

FELLING TREES

Old timers will be surprised to learn that the standard way of notching a tree has been re-thought. Originally, it was recommended that a 30- to 40-degree notch should be cut on the side of the tree in the direction of the anticipated fall. This has been revised to a 60- to 90-degree notch which makes it less likely that the tree will snap erratically when it falls, closing the gap. Be aware that the wind can push the tree in the opposite direction than where it was anticipated to fall. Pick a calm day or drop the tree in the direction of the wind. Keep a couple of plastic wedges handy in case the tree pinches the cutter bar, and have an ax handy to pound the wedges into the saw cut (kerf).

Correct Notches

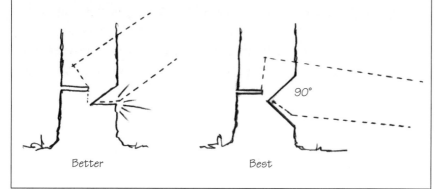

Better   Best

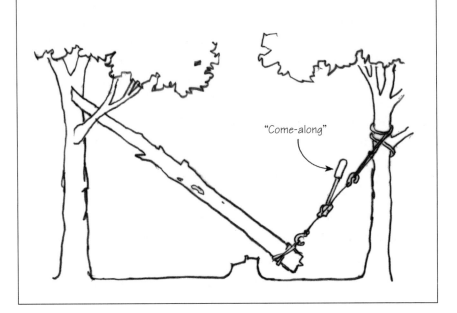

Choose a path for the tree to fall where it won't get hung up in another tree. This is sometimes not as easy as it sounds, especially in a dense forest. If your tree does get hung up, use a "come-along" to winch the tree down.

"Come-along"

Transporting Logs

Transporting the logs to the building site may be the most difficult part of the job. Logs can weigh 10 to 20 pounds per foot depending on diameter and species. One solution is to use a horse. Don't laugh! Modern technology has not found a way to skid logs out of a dense forest better than having a horse pull them. Any vehicle strong enough to pull logs requires some sort of a path or roadway, which requires additional trees to be cut down to provide access for the vehicle. A horse, on the other hand, can maneuver its way between trees, rocks and stumps. There is a horse especially bred for this purpose. Try asking at a local farm if you can hire a horse and driver to help you haul out the logs. Farmers are less busy in the winter and may be more available for work.

To make pulling the logs over the ground easier, you may need a log "boat," or skid, to keep the butt end from digging into the

Log "Boat"

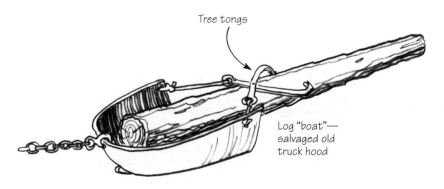

Tree tongs

Log "boat"—
salvaged old
truck hood

ground. One method is to use a salvaged truck hood, with a 3/4" eye bolt securely welded to the front end.

Log Wheeler

If a horse and driver are not available, you can build your own log wheeler from two pieces of 3/4" pressure-treated plywood and some pieces of galvanized pipe. Glue and screw two 4'x4' pieces of plywood together and cut out the two wheels. Cut 8" diameter holes in the plywood wheels to make them lighter without diminishing their strength. The wheels are made purposely tall so the axle will pass over rocks and stumps without difficulty. The wheels are joined together by a bridge made up of two pieces of 2x4s, bolted to the outer pipe. The axle is held between the 2x4 and 2x10 and consists of two pieces of pipe, one fitting inside the other. Two 1 1/2" flanges hold the axles to the plywood wheels, with two 1 1/4" caps placed at the ends. A saddle of wedge-shaped 2x4s is screwed to the top to hold the log in the center during transporting. In practice, you lift up the log and rest it in the saddle so that it is equally balanced, front to end, and tie it to the rig. Two men can then pull the log over rough terrain with comparative ease, allowing the wheels to take all the weight.

If you are moving logs during the warmer months and your logs are upstream from your building site, you might consider tying them into rafts and floating them downstream or tying them between two canoes and paddling them to your site.

Log Wheeler

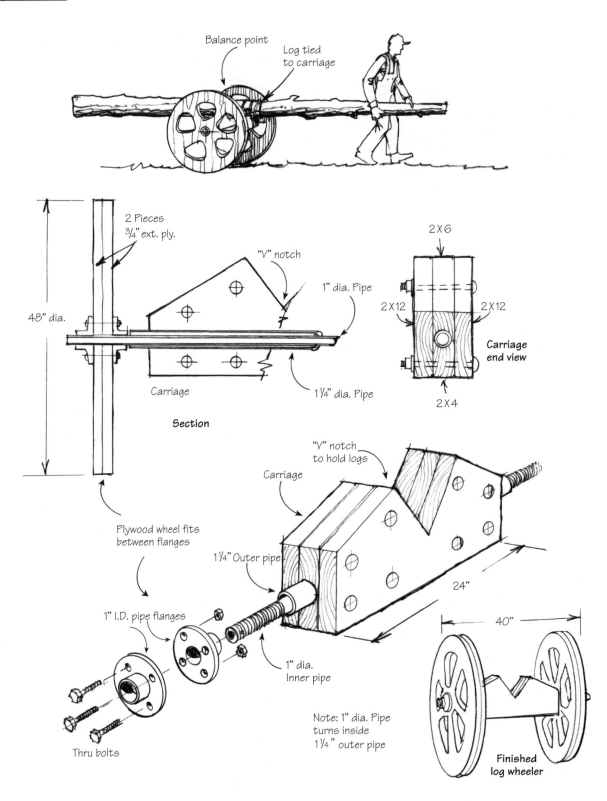

Balance point

Log tied to carriage

2 Pieces ¾" ext. ply.

"V" notch

1" dia. Pipe

48" dia.

Carriage

1¼" dia. Pipe

Section

2 X 6

2 X 12   2 X 12

Carriage end view

2 X 4

"V" notch to hold logs

Carriage

1¼" Outer pipe

24"

Plywood wheel fits between flanges

1" I.D. pipe flanges

1" dia. Inner pipe

40"

Thru bolts

Note: 1" dia. Pipe turns inside 1¼" outer pipe

Finished log wheeler

Working with Logs

Peeling

Peeling is best done in the spring when the sap is running. You may be tempted to omit this step and leave the bark on the logs. There are

Some Tools Used in Building with Logs

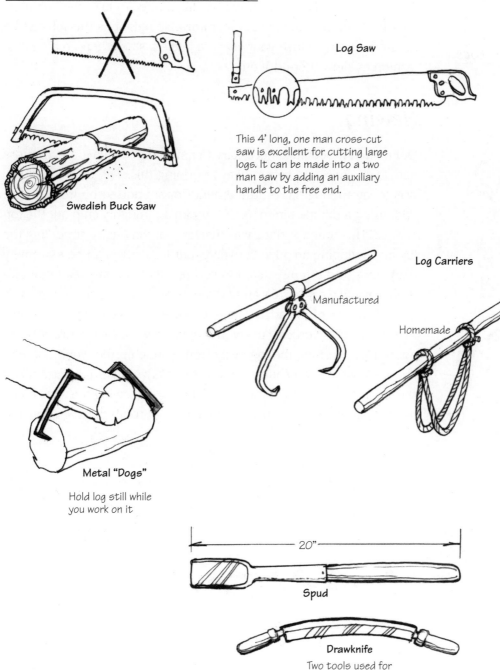

Log Saw

This 4' long, one man cross-cut saw is excellent for cutting large logs. It can be made into a two man saw by adding an auxiliary handle to the free end.

Swedish Buck Saw

Log Carriers

Manufactured

Homemade

Metal "Dogs"

Hold log still while you work on it

20"

Spud

Drawknife

Two tools used for taking bark off logs

several reasons why it is important to remove the bark. Once the logs are cut and start to dry out, they shrink and begin to loose their bark, resulting in a shaggy appearance. During this time, the bark makes a perfect place for insects to nest and start colonies in the wood. Removing the bark early on prevents this from happening. How you peel the logs depends on the type of wood you are working with. White pine, for instance, can be peeled by cutting the bark length-wise down the log and using pliers to strip it off. Other types of thick bark can be chiseled off using a commercially available "spud" (see Sources) and finishing it off with a drawknife. To take the strain off your back, elevate the log to a comfortable height as this job can be time-consuming. Once your logs are peeled, stack them in a criblike fashion to allow them dry out.

Hewing

Quite often it becomes necessary to hew a log to give it one or more flat sides. There are several ways of doing this. The traditional way was to lay the log flat on the ground (or supported by iron "dogs") and, using a double bitted ax or a broad ax, roughly chip out the top surface. This rough surface was then smoothed out by straddling the log and swinging an adze between your legs. This can be extremely dangerous and often resulted in severe cuts. We have read that old-timers would wear barrels around their legs to avoid being cut by mis-guided strokes of the adze. There is, however, a safer way to do this: first make short vertical cuts with a chain saw approximately 3" to 4" apart, then, turning the log away from you, chip the wood out with an ax. Finishing can still be done with an adze but not by straddling the log. Instead, stand to the side of the log and swing the adze much like you would a golf club, allowing plenty of room between you and

Peeling & Drying the Logs

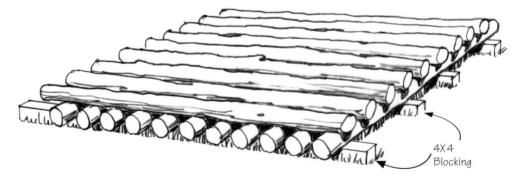

4X4
Blocking

Hewing (Squaring Off) Logs

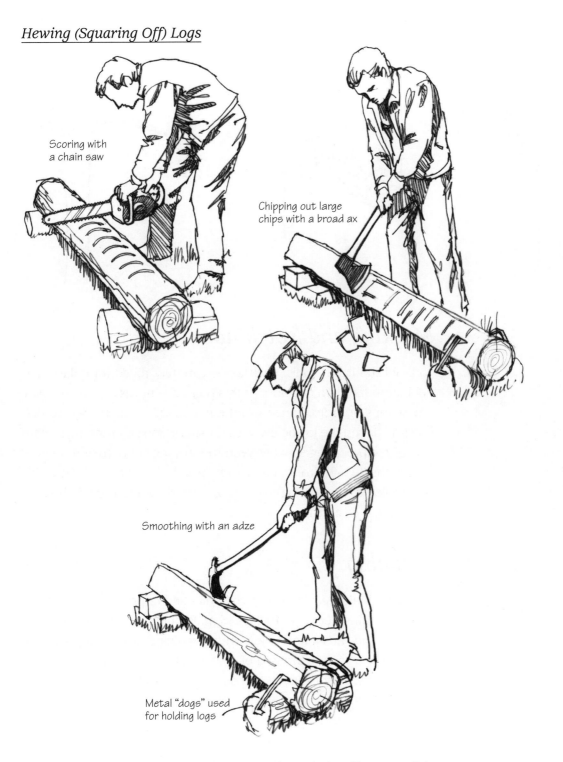

Scoring with a chain saw

Chipping out large chips with a broad ax

Smoothing with an adze

Metal "dogs" used for holding logs

the adze head, in case one of your strokes skids off. You will be amazed at how quickly you can remove large quantities of wood using this method. An 8' fresh oak log may take less than an hour to hew four sides.

Hewing Tools

Double bitted ax
for scoring and
removing chips

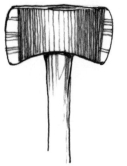

Broad ax used for
hewing to a line

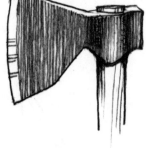

Adze for finishing
and smoothing

Marking and Notching

To build the cabin walls, each log is carefully rolled into place and held temporarily in position. At this point it is necessary to cut away any bumps or protrusions from the underside of the top log so that it will lie flat on the log below. This is usually done by running a chain saw or reciprocating saw between the two logs until they fit together (see the Two-Bedroom Log Cabin later in this chapter). Once this is completed, the top log is scribed or marked and the notch is cut out, using a chain saw or an adze.

Chinking

If you are building a log cabin you will need to provide some caulking or chinking between the logs to make them air tight and to keep out bugs and mosquitoes. How much caulking or chinking you will need depends on the amount of space there is between the logs. For instance, the Swedish cope and some of the milled log types of log construction will require only a couple of thin beads of caulking applied with a caulking gun. On the other hand, some hand-hewn log cabins may have 4" spaces between the logs, then requiring major chinking. Early log cabin builders used moss stuffed in-between the logs. This held up pretty well since it was flexible and compressed as the logs settled. A modern-day alternative is a 6" wide Fiberglas sill sealer sold commercially at most building supply yards

Homemade Marking Gauge

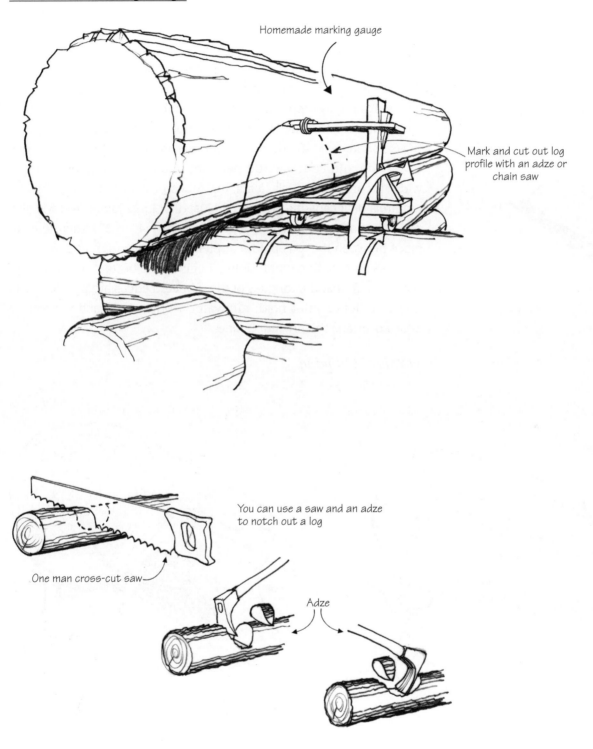

Homemade marking gauge

Mark and cut out log profile with an adze or chain saw

You can use a saw and an adze to notch out a log

One man cross-cut saw

Adze

and used extensively to build houses. This is a good choice if you are using unseasoned logs as they will undoubtedly settle and shrink over the first two to three years at which time you can apply a permanent type of chinking.

There are several choices of permanent type chinking. One solution is to nail 6" wide strips of wire mesh to the logs and fill the gap with a regular cement sand mix. Another solution is to purchase a manufactured elastic chinking material called "Log Jam" by SASH-CO (see Sources). The manufacturer boasts that their product is able to expand and contract 100 per cent and can span gaps up to 2" wide. It comes in regular caulking tubes or 5 gallon drums, which require a bulk caulking gun and are used for large joints. You will also need plastic foam backer rods, which come 1/4" to 2" in diameter, to place between the logs before applying the caulking material.

As with all horizontal siding, begin at the bottom and work up, making sure that the tongues of the rabbeted edges are positioned so they will deflect, not hold, rainwater. Notice that each successive board overlaps the preceding one.

Guide for Cutting Log Ends Square

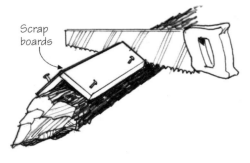

Scrap boards

Forms of Chinking

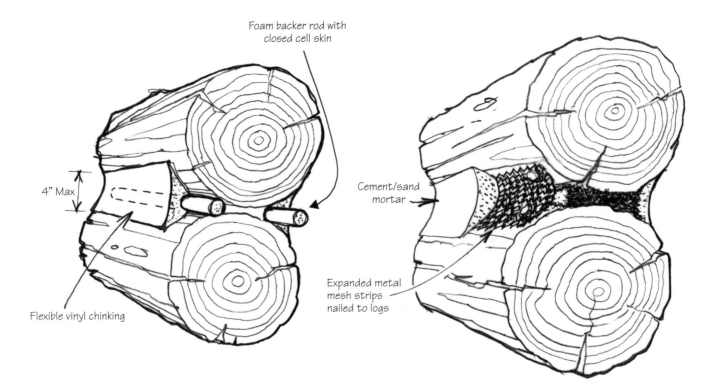

Foam backer rod with closed cell skin

4" Max

Flexible vinyl chinking

Cement/sand mortar

Expanded metal mesh strips nailed to logs

Don Gesinger

Photo: Don Gesinger

We first saw this octagonal log cabin in an old issue of *Shelter II* and contacted Don Gesinger, the designer and builder, who lives and works in northern British Columbia. Don lived in a tent during the six months that it took him to build the cabin. Aside from the logs, which he found, cut and peeled on the site, the only materials that Don needed to purchase were the 2x6 tongue and groove decking, 1x6 roof boards, reflecting foil, used glass windows, flashing nails and caulking.

The cabin, which rests on a dry stone foundation, required approximately eighty 14', straight, peeled logs for the walls and fifty 5" diameter logs for the rafters. The roof is covered with hand-split cedar shakes, and the front door and deck are protected by a large overhanging roof. In the years following construction, several bedrooms were added to the basic structure. Twenty years later, Don still uses his cabin as a getaway studio where he can work without the interruption of phones and faxes, drawing up plans for much larger log homes, for a long list of clients.

Two-Bedroom Log Cabin

For cabin dwellers who prefer relaxing while roughing it, this comfortable, yet traditional log cabin is a perfect size. It is cozy enough for a couple to escape to for a weekend alone and contains an extra bedroom in case they care to invite a guest. The two bedrooms are intentionally small, keeping them snugly warm and economizing on heating. All the rooms have a minimum of two windows, which permits light to enter and provides cross ventilation in the summer. Unlike the bedrooms, the bathroom is spacious, allowing for luxurious hot baths on cold winter evenings. It can be modified in many ways to suit your taste. We chose a free-standing bathtub to go with the rustic look of the cabin, however, for a more contemporary look, there is plenty of room to install a tiled spa. The window above the sink can be eliminated since there are two others and a mirrored wall/cabinet put in its place. Since guests will be sharing this bathroom, a "knock first" rule can avoid an embarrassing situation. In our weekend home, a closed door signifies "occupied," while an open door means "come right in." Your friends (especially those with no weekend cabin of their own) may say this design lacks bedrooms and should have two bathrooms. Keep in mind, this is a cabin to escape to, not a resort for entertaining and cleaning up after guests.

The combination living room/dining room/kitchen is dominated by a large stone fireplace with a massive oak mantel. The kitchen area is small but efficient. Perishable food can be stored in an under-counter refrigerator and non-perishable food in a corner cabinet over the sink. Cooking is done using a gas or electric oven. A 48" diameter dining table is nestled in a bay window and surrounded by a bench large enough for unexpected visitors to sit around and drink coffee. A generous 8' deep covered porch extends the full length of the cabin, providing a perfect place for friends to sit outside and watch the sun set over the lake. The covered deck also provides an excellent place to store canoes or firewood.

Above and to the rear of the living room is an open loft, which can be used for storage. In a pinch, it can become a cozy, warm sleeping loft for kids or extra guests, as it is easily accessible by means of a pull-out ladder.

Materials

The following plans show the cabin being built using 9" diameter peeled logs, however, the cabin can be constructed out of conventional lumber, substituting 2x6 or 2x4 framing for the logs. We prefer to see rough sawn shiplapped northern pine nailed horizontally to flat 2x4 furring, attached to the interior of the log wall.

If you plan on finishing the interior log walls with paneling, make sure the interior walls are plumb and allow the exterior walls to be irregular if necessary. Not only does rough sawn northern pine look good, it also gives off a wonderful woodsy aroma that will last for years.

If the site for your cabin is sloped, you may want to bring in heavy equipment to level the land or to excavate for a poured concrete foundation. Or, you may prefer building the cabin on the slope, making the posts or piers taller at the bottom of the hill. Hopefully, you have found a flat site which will require only locust posts or masonry piers to support the log sills . After clearing the site for your cabin, lay out the footprint and build your corner piers. Make a 24' long, 4 1/2"x9 1/4" center girder by nailing three layers of 2x10 together. Be sure to stagger the joints. Support the girder by providing masonry supports every 8' or adjustable floor jacks embedded in masonry piers.

Two-Bedroom Log Cabin Side View & Section

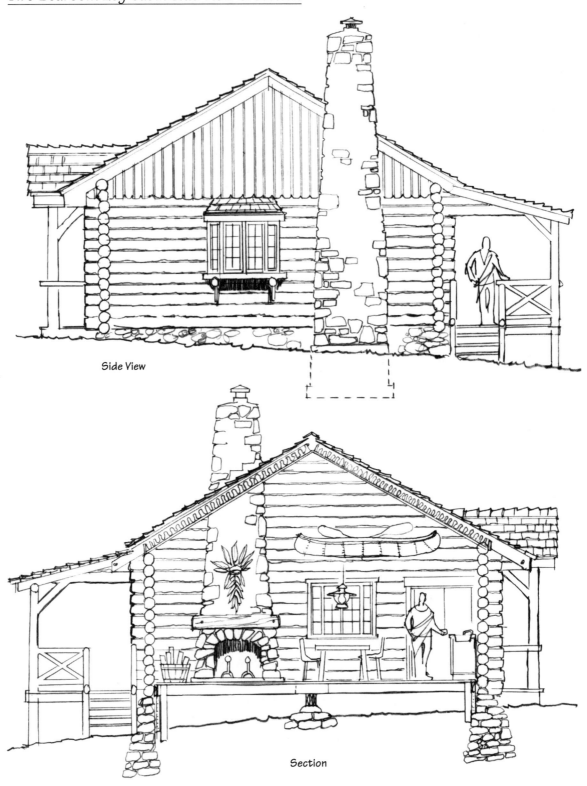

Side View

Section

Floor Plan

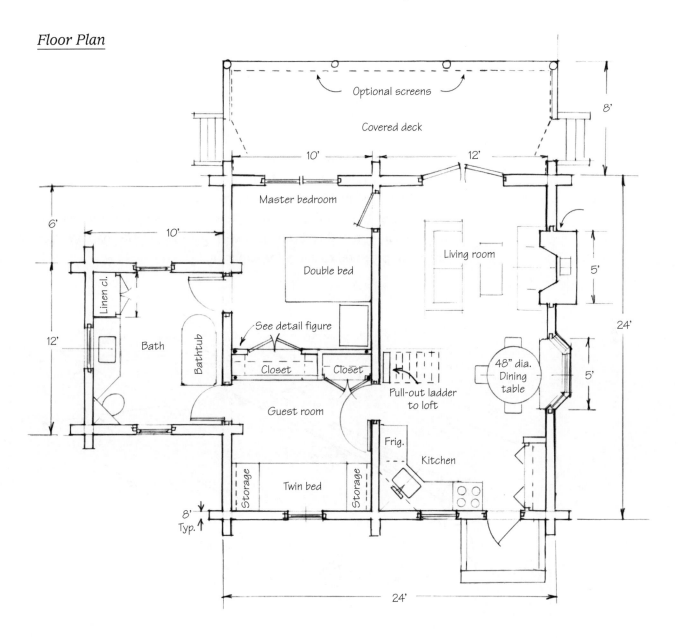

Foundation

Cut and lay the front and rear sill logs. Fill underneath them with tightly fitted stones, backed on the interior side with 2" Styrofoam rigid insulation, 2' wide, supported by 2x4 posts. It may be necessary to provide a narrow trench for the bottom of the 2" rigid insulation so that the full width of 24" can be used. This will keep the cold out and protect the pipes from freezing. Provide 8"x16" vents on each foundation wall as required by code.

Notch and install the next pair of logs perpendicular to the first logs. Fill in below the logs with insulation and stones. Cut and nail a 2x10 header to the flattened inside of the sill logs. Cut and nail the 2x10 floor joists, spaced 16" apart, to butt against the header and attach them with metal joist hangers. For added support, hammer the 2x4 post supports into the ground before nailing them to the 2x10 joists, spaced 16" apart. Note: If logs have to be spliced, use a lap joint and provide a pier under the joint.

Use 2" galvanized deck screws to attach 3/4" plywood panel subflooring to the joists. Using screws enables you to remove the flooring later on to do plumbing or wiring. Leave an 1/8" gap between sheets of plywood to allow for expansion.

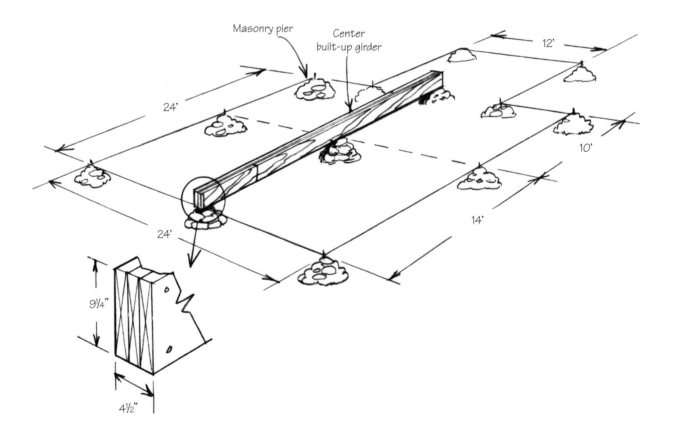

Log Cabin Foundation

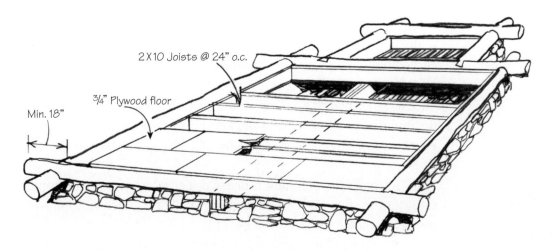

2 X 10 Joists @ 24" o.c.

3/4" Plywood floor

Min. 18"

Section Detail

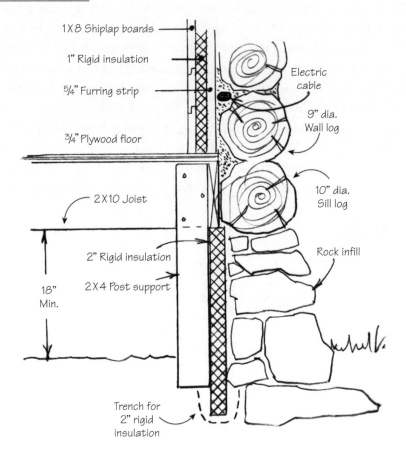

1 X 8 Shiplap boards

1" Rigid insulation

5/4" Furring strip

3/4" Plywood floor

2 X 10 Joist

2" Rigid insulation

2 X 4 Post support

18" Min.

Trench for 2" rigid insulation

Electric cable

9" dia. Wall log

10" dia. Sill log

Rock infill

Log Walls

As you begin to build the walls, make a note of which end of each log is thicker and alternate them as you build. If any of the logs are curved (crowned), position them bowed side up and, if necessary, make kerf cuts on the tops of the logs to help them straighten out once a load is placed on them. Some log home builders disagree with this method and believe that the kerf cuts promote rot. To help prevent this from happening, carefully fill any gaps with clear silicone caulking.

To make the chinking process easier later on, provide something for the chinking cement to grip by nailing 3" wide strips of wire mesh between each layer of logs.

Assuming that you have a plentiful supply of peeled, seasoned, straight, 9" diameter logs, place them in piles around the four sides of the foundation. To lift the logs into place, build a simple ramp out of two inclined scaffolding boards and roll the logs up, using two ropes. Bevel the tops of the two ramp boards. To prevent the logs from rolling back down the ramp, cut two pieces of 2x4 and hammer several nails through them at an angle. Place these stop blocks behind the log as you roll it up the ramp, in case you want to stop and rest.

If you are covering the interior log walls with paneling, make sure the logs are plumb on the inside. If the logs are to be seen on both the inside and outside, center them directly over each other for stability. To help keep the walls plumb, build two triangular braces out of 2x4s and temporarily nail them to the wall. Place a wooden

Curved Logs

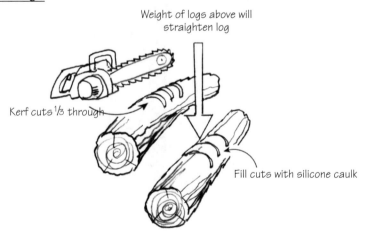

Weight of logs above will straighten log

Kerf cuts ⅓ through

Fill cuts with silicone caulk

Log Cabin Construction

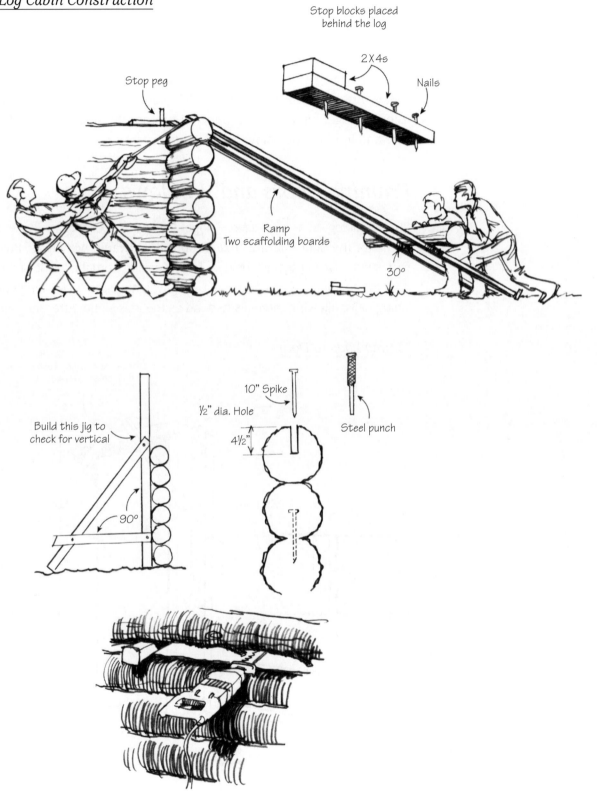

Stop blocks placed
behind the log

2 X 4s

Nails

Stop peg

Ramp
Two scaffolding boards

30°

Build this jig to
check for vertical

90°

½" dia. Hole

4½"

10" Spike

Steel punch

wedge between the logs to create a gap and use a reciprocating saw to cut off any bumps or protrusions that prevent the logs from fitting together snugly. If any gaps appear between the logs, fill them with Fiberglas sill sealer strips.

Each layer of logs is spiked to the layer below it, using 10" long spikes. Attach them by drilling a 1/2" diameter hole, 4 1/2" deep, using an auger bit and a steel punch. Hammer the spike through the hole and into the log below (see illustration).

Framing Doors and Windows

Cut the sill log off at a 15-degree slope where the door will go. Make a frame for the door out of 2x10s and brace the frame with 1x2s. Butt each successive log against the door frame, nailing from the inside of the door frame into the end of the log. Use only lightweight 3 1/2" long finishing nails, allowing the nails to bend as the logs settle. After the logs

Joining Logs to Doors

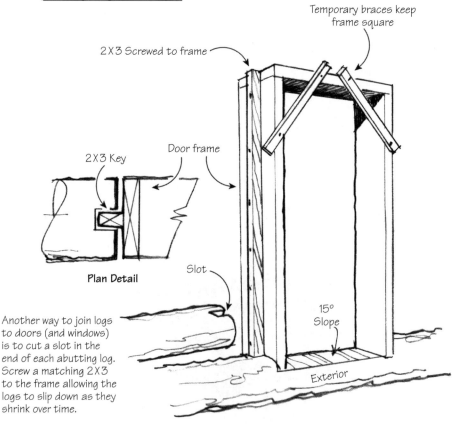

Temporary braces keep frame square

2 X 3 Screwed to frame

Door frame

2 X 3 Key

Plan Detail

Slot

15° Slope

Another way to join logs to doors (and windows) is to cut a slot in the end of each abutting log. Screw a matching 2 X 3 to the frame allowing the logs to slip down as they shrink over time.

Exterior

have fully dried out, nail spikes through the frames and into the log ends to hold them permanently. Caulk any gaps as you work. Make sure that the thickness of your door frame is the same thickness as your logs. Use the same procedure for building the window sills. Since the logs will settle, leave 2" to 3" above the doors and windows and cover the open spaces with casing boards.

Second Floor Loft

When the wall height reaches approximately 8', begin building the loft. First construct an adjustable load-bearing wall partition in the center of the cabin, running 11' from the living room to the bathroom. This wall should line up with the load-bearing girder under the cabin floor. Since log walls have a tendency to dry out and shrink over time, use adjustable house jacks inside the partition wall to compensate for this shrinkage. These are the same type of jacks used in the crawl space, but longer. As the cabin settles, you can reduce the height of the second floor by unscrewing the jacks, a little at a time.

Gable Walls

The gabled wall ends of the cabin are framed with dimensional 2x6 lumber. It is easiest to frame the two gable units while they are laying flat on the ground and lift them up into position over the end walls. Nail cross pieces ("cats") between the studs and vertical slab boards across the gable. A 2' overhang not only looks good but also protects the logs from rain. To provide for this, run 2x10 lookout boards from the inboard rafter to the outboard "fly" rafter. To cover the gap left between the lookout rafters, install blocking.

Adjusting Load-Bearing Partitions

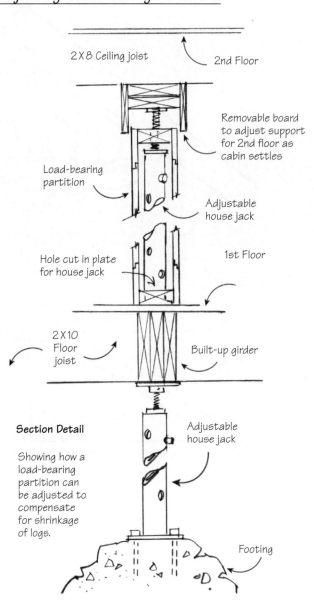

2 X 8 Ceiling joist

2nd Floor

Removable board to adjust support for 2nd floor as cabin settles

Load-bearing partition

Adjustable house jack

1st Floor

Hole cut in plate for house jack

2 X 10 Floor joist

Built-up girder

Section Detail

Showing how a load-bearing partition can be adjusted to compensate for shrinkage of logs.

Adjustable house jack

Footing

Roof Framing

Frame the roof with trusses made out of 2x8s and logs joined together and spaced 4' apart. You will need at least two long logs for the bottom of the two unsupported trusses that span the living room.

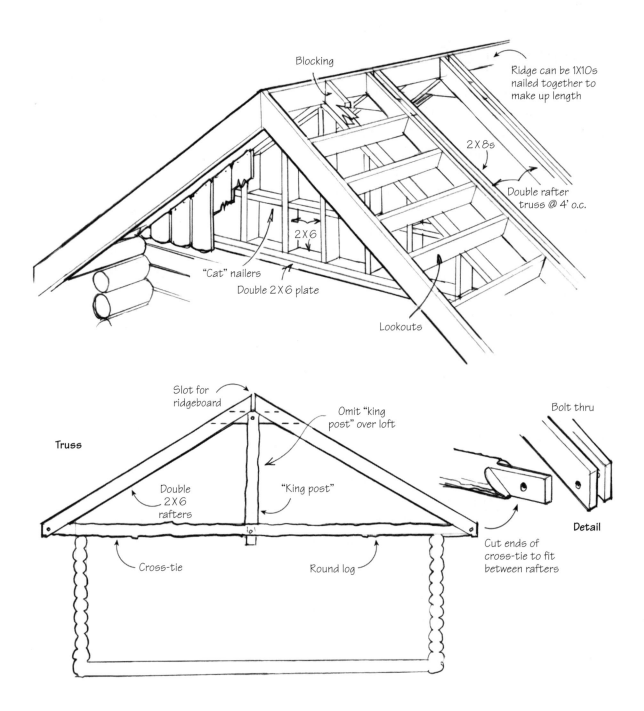

Blocking

Ridge can be 1X10s nailed together to make up length

2 X 8s

Double rafter truss @ 4' o.c.

2 X 6

"Cat" nailers

Double 2 X 6 plate

Lookouts

Truss

Slot for ridgeboard

Omit "king post" over loft

"King post"

Double 2 X 6 rafters

Cross-tie

Round log

Bolt thru

Detail

Cut ends of cross-tie to fit between rafters

These trusses should each be reinforced in the middle by a vertical "king post" that extends down from the peak to the middle of the cross-tie.

Roof Decking

The roof is constructed from 2x6 tongue and groove decking, nailed to the trusses, 4' on center. Cover the roof with either asphalt or cedar shingles, hand-split cedar shakes or galvanized sheet metal roofing material. To conserve heat, insulate the roof using R-30 Fiberglas batts stapled between the rafters. Use a 2x2 spacer between each pair of rafters, to provide space for the finished ceiling material. The spacer should extend below the rafters the same thickness as the ceiling material. The ceiling material butts up to either side of the spacer and is nailed to the rafters.

Ceiling Detail

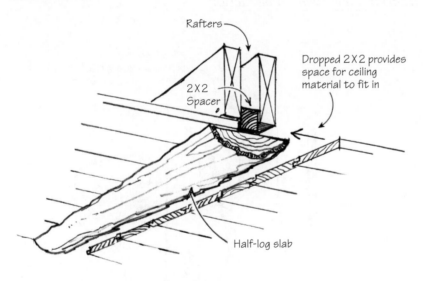

Ceiling Insulation

The ceiling is insulated with R-30 Fiberglas batts, stapled between the rafters and covered with 1/2" drywall or shiplapped 1x8 boards. To maintain the rustic look and to hide the sloping vertical joints, nail half-log slabs to the spacers. If you are using plaster drywall for the finished ceiling material, skim coat it with a 1/4" thick mixture of 50 per cent Structolite and 50 per cent drywall spackle.

Interior Walls

If you wish, leave the interior walls exposed, showing off the beautiful log craftsmanship. Some communities may require you to insulate the interior walls, which means furring them out with vertical strips, insulating and covering them with plaster wallboard or vertical or horizontal tongue and groove boards. How wide the vertical furring is depends on the thickness of the insulation you want to use. In this case, we relied, for the most part, on the logs themselves to block out the majority of the wind and cold, adding only 1" of insulation. Nail the 5/4" x 3" furring strips to the log wall on 16" centers. If the wall is not perfectly plumb, shim out the furring strips with pieces of shingles.

Interior View Wall Construction

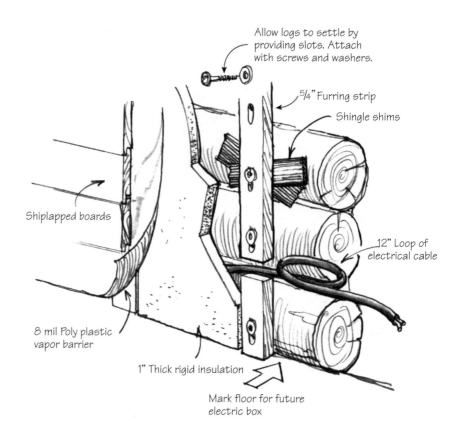

Allow logs to settle by providing slots. Attach with screws and washers.

5/4" Furring strip

Shingle shims

Shiplapped boards

12" Loop of electrical cable

8 mil Poly plastic vapor barrier

1" Thick rigid insulation

Mark floor for future electric box

Fill the space between the furring strips with 1" rigid insulation and caulk any gaps that may occur. Cover the walls with 8 mil poly plastic sheeting stapled to the furring strips. Leave a space, 6" above the floor for electric wiring. Tip: Even if you don't anticipate having electric in the future, it is still a good idea to run electric cables throughout the house to avoid ripping out the wall if you change your mind. The easiest way to make a space for the electric cable is to run the furring strips and insulation all the way to the floor and cut the horizontal groove out with a circular saw, making two passes. Leave 12" of extra electric cable every place you anticipate having an electric outlet and leave a mark on the finished wall where the ends of the wires are buried. Nail the shiplapped boards to the wall, starting from the bottom. If you are having a professional electrician wire your house, wait before putting the wallboard on. You may have to have a building inspector and electrical inspector check the wiring.

The bay window should be ordered in advance and set in place during the construction of the wall. Instructions come with the window and should be followed carefully. To support the bay window at the bottom, notch out and install two legs, protruding from the side of the cabin. Provide two smaller logs to brace the ends of the support logs.

Fireplace and Chimney

Leave an opening approximately 5' high and 6' wide for the fireplace. It is best to have a mason build this at the same time you build the cabin, so you can coordinate where the chimney will cut through the roof. (Bear in mind that the code says that no structural member can be within 2" of the chimney.) The chimney and fireplace must rest on a solid concrete footing since they support a 4" thick concrete hearth in front of the fireplace opening. It also should be tied into the log walls with metal ties and should be flashed where the chimney emerges from the roof. The chimney should have a spark arrestor cap at the top not only to prevent fires but also to prevent squirrels from entering the cabin when you are not there. The fireplace mantel is an important focal point. Pick one out that frames your fireplace well, as you and your guests will spend a lot of time looking at it.

Cabin Reflections

Whatever a house is to the heart and body of man – refuge, comfort, luxury
– surely it is as much or more to the spirit.   Mary Oliver   *Winter Hours*

CABIN DESIGNS

I often start work in the dark and when the pink glow of sunrise filters through the trees this is the prettiest place on earth. And it is truly a quiet place to work. Jim put two big drawers in the desk, but because he made one of them himself and salvaged the other from a previous job, they are of different sizes and styles. When I pointed this out to him, he replied, "So what? When you're working at the desk you can't look at them both at the same time." That really makes it a country cabin.

—Wallis Lawrence, writer

Helen's Writing Cabin

Henry David Thoreau had one, Virginia Woolf had one, George Bernard Shaw had one—why not you? Although you may not be a world famous writer, you still deserve a place of your own, some distance from the house, where you can spend time, uninterrupted, contemplating, working on a meaningful project or just relaxing and reading a favorite book. Our good friend Helen asked us to design just such a writing cabin for her home in Vermont. The same cabin design could work just as well as a painting or pottery studio.

To begin the design process, we took a photograph at the base of a hill not far from the main house where Helen wanted the cabin to be built. Because of the hilly terrain, we decided to design a cabin on posts, as opposed to using stepped, masonry foundation, which would be

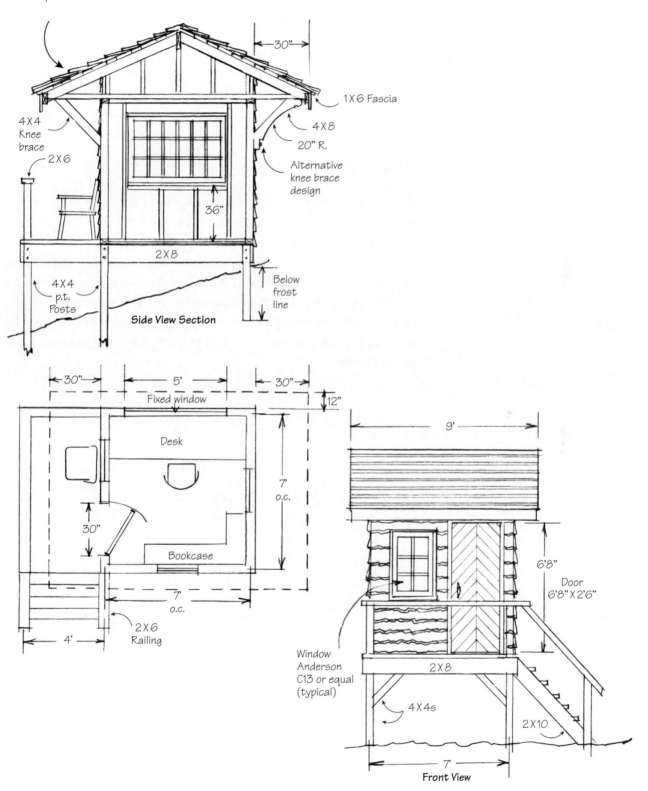

Hand-split shakes

30"

1 X 6 Fascia

4 X 4
Knee
brace

2 X 6

4 X 8
20" R.

Alternative
knee brace
design

36"

2 X 8

Below
frost
line

4 X 4
p.t.
Posts

Side View Section

30"   5'   30"

12"

Fixed window

Desk

7
o.c.

30"

Bookcase

7
o.c.

4'

2 X 6
Railing

9'

6'8"

Door
6'8" X 2'6"

Window
Anderson
C13 or equal
(typical)

2 X 8

4 X 4s

2 X 10

7

Front View

more costly and time-consuming. We then cut out and superimposed three different designs over the photograph so Helen could compare how each design would look in the same setting. We all agreed on the design shown, which contains elements of all three original designs. This small cabin, just big enough for one person to work comfortably at a writing table, is situated only 50' from the main house. It faces mountains, lending a sense of privacy and solitude. One window is larger than the rest, providing a view of the surrounding pine forest.

Interior

Design the interior of your cabin to suit your needs. For instance, you may want to insulate the walls and cover the insulation with an interesting paneling, or you may prefer to paint the walls, ceiling and floor white. For inexpensive table tops, you can cut down flush doors, available at your local lumber yard. Filing cabinets and book shelves are also a must for a writer. If you choose to run a power line from your house, you can have electricity with all of its benefits and drawbacks, or you may want to stick to a gas lantern and retain a more rustic environment.

Foundation

Dig four holes below the frost line, 7' apart (center to center) and place four 4x4 pressure-treated posts in the holes. The posts should extend at least 8' above the ground, measured from the highest point of land. This means that the downhill posts will have to be longer in order to reach the same height as the uphill posts. Install the posts but do not backfill until later. Nail two 12', 2x8 beams to the 4x4 posts, making sure both beams are level and parallel with each other. Allow the side beams to overlap, 1 1/2" past the rear posts. Cut a 2x8, 7' 3 1/2" long

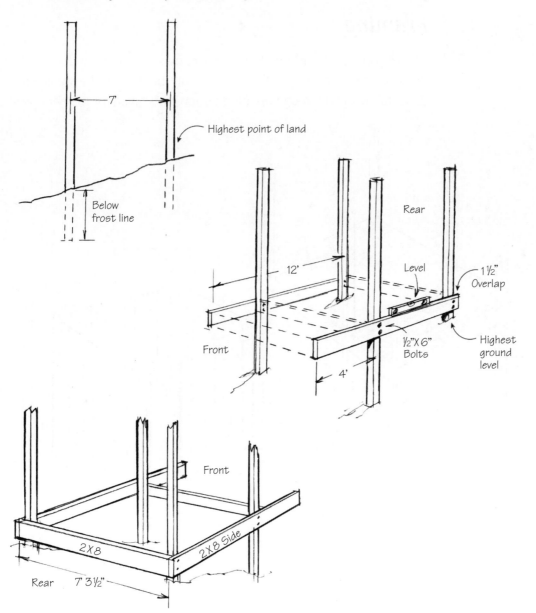

and nail it to the two rear posts and in between the 1 1/2" overhanging 2x8 side beams. Do the same thing to the front posts. Cut a third 2x8, 7' 3 1/2" long, and nail it between the two side beams. Drop a plumb line down through the front inside corners of the floor frame to the ground and dig two more holes below the frost line. Install two additional 4x4 pressure-treated posts. Make sure they extend at least 30" above the floor frame. Cut and nail a center 2x8 joist between the two side beams. Cover the deck with 2x4s, spaced 1/4" apart and cover the interior with 2x6 tongue and groove decking.

Framing

Before you begin framing, buy the windows and door, to determine what the rough openings for these should be. Frame the walls with 2x4s, following the rough opening dimensions given for the windows

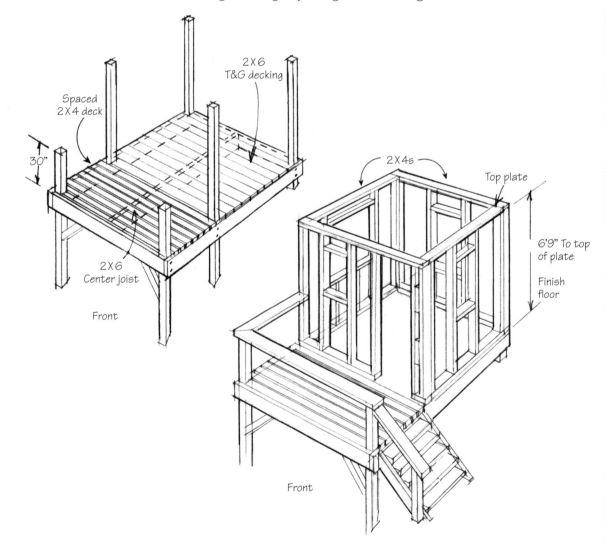

and door. Build the gable ends as shown. Note that the two inclining 2x4 top pieces do not touch at the peak, allowing a space for a 2x6 ridgepole. The 2x4s are held together by a 3/4" thick plywood gusset plate. Cut out a 1 1/2"x5 1/2" notch in the top middle of the gusset plate, to hold the ridgepole (see illustration). Nail the two pre-framed gable ends to the to wall plates so that they each protrude 30" on the front and rear.

Gable End Construction

Cut a piece of 2x6 for the ridgepole so that it protrudes 1' on each side to provide an overhang for the roof. Cut and install two 2x4s the same length for the front and rear fascia supports and nail them to the gable ends.

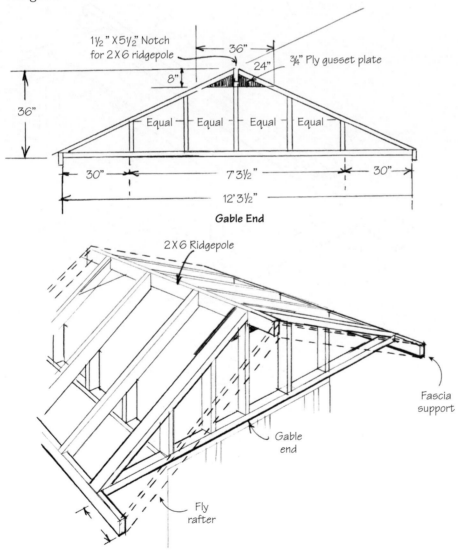

Gable End

Cut eight 2x4 rafters to fit between the top ridgepole and the 2x4 fascia supports. To do this, temporarily nail an 8' 2x4 to the end of the ridgepole and the fascia support and mark the angles with a pencil. Cut and screw the rafters to the ridgepole and fascia support.

Cut and install vertical nailers, reaching from the top plate to the underside of the rafters. The siding will be nailed to these nailers. It may be necessary to block between the rafters to help keep out the cold air. If you are using your cabin only during the warm months, cover this opening with mosquito netting, allowing for ventilation while keeping out the bugs.

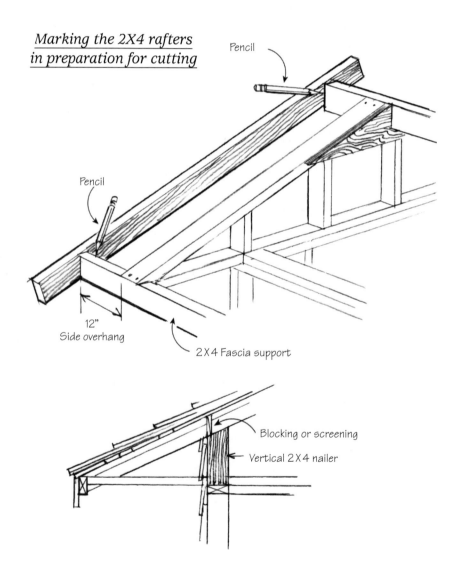

Marking the 2X4 rafters in preparation for cutting

Pencil

Pencil

12"
Side overhang

2 X 4 Fascia support

Blocking or screening

Vertical 2 X 4 nailer

Roofing

Nail a 1x6 across the top and at the tail end of the rafters, allowing a 1" overhang. Butt and nail two additional 1x4s above the first one. Continue nailing 1x4s, spaced 10" on center from each other, to the top of the roof. Cover the 1x4s with 24" hand-split red cedar shingles, nailed over 30 lb. felt (tar paper).

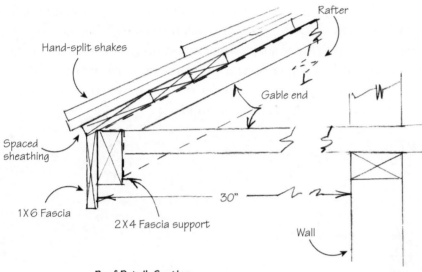

Roof Detail: Section

Siding

The slab siding we recommend for this cabin could be used for many of the cabins in this book. It is relatively cheap and easy to install. However, you will not find it sold in a lumber yard, only at saw mills. Look in the yellow pages for the saw mill nearest you or contact your department of forestry. Have the saw mill cut off one edge square, leaving the boards the same size and allowing for a cleaner look on the inside of the cabin.

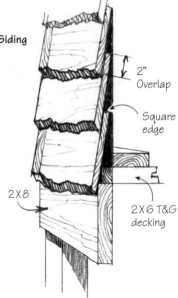

Rustic Siding

Pyramid Cabin

Generally, we recommend that a cabin be designed to blend in with the surrounding terrain and environment. Since it is almost impossible to build a structure that blends in completely with its natural surroundings, why not do the opposite and build a pyramid cabin? Here is a structure that stands out magnificently, revealing its own distinct personality and strikingly dynamic shape. Imagine trekking through woods, miles from civilization and suddenly discovering a shimmering perfectly geometrical pyramid. One of the first man-made dwellings was made by propping fallen trees together at the top, resulting in a pyramidal shape. The most famous pyramids, of course, were built by the Egyptians, who entrusted the souls and possessions of their dead to them, and even today there is much written about the metaphysical properties of the pyramid.

Pyramid Cabin Plans

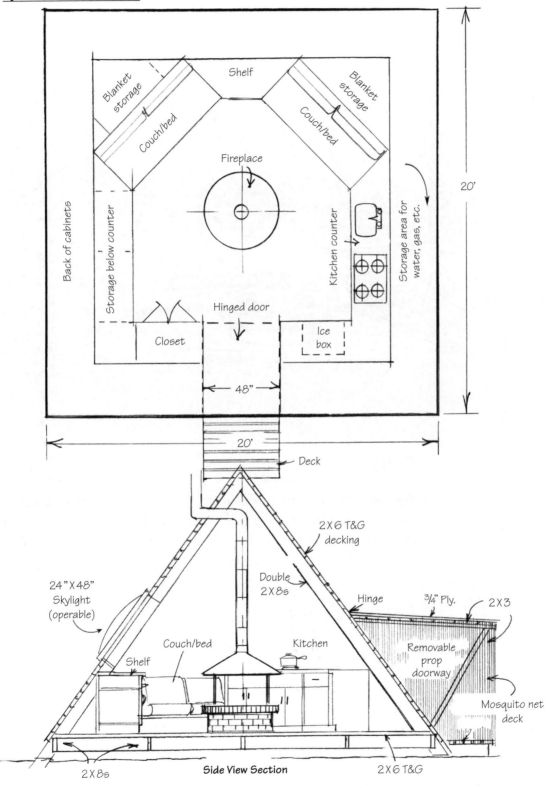

Blanket storage

Shelf

Blanket storage

Couch/bed

Couch/bed

Fireplace

Back of cabinets

Storage below counter

Kitchen counter

Storage area for water, gas, etc.

Hinged door

Closet

Ice box

48"

20'

20'

20'

Deck

2 X 6 T&G decking

Double 2 X 8s

Hinge

3/4" Ply.

2 X 3

24" X 48" Skylight (operable)

Shelf

Couch/bed

Kitchen

Removable prop doorway

Mosquito net deck

2 X 8s

Side View Section

2 X 6 T&G

Pyramid Cabin Interior

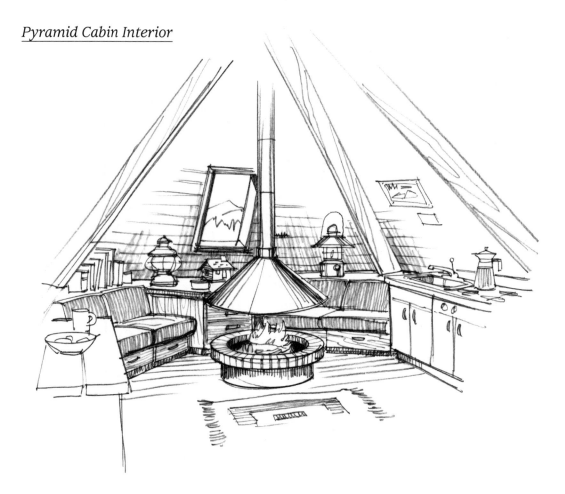

Footings

The four corner footings are simply four holes dug below the frost line and filled with concrete or a mixture of cement and stones. A "U" shaped metal bracket should be secured to each footing before attaching the 3x8 corner beams.

Corner Beams

The final 3"x8" dimension of each of the four corner beams (made using a doubled 2x8) should be approximately 18' long. The easiest way of making up this length is to nail together shorter lengths of 2x8s and stagger the joints. Build the first pair of corner beams on the ground and raise them, using props to hold them in place. Lay the second and third corner beams against the first pair and nail them together. Reinforce the top connection by tying the ends together with a 1/4" wire cable.

Corner Beams

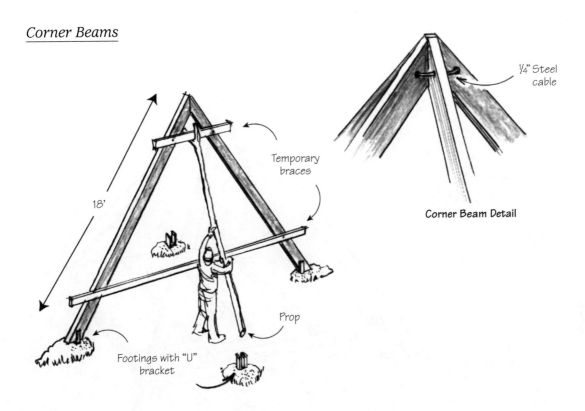

1/4" Steel cable

Temporary braces

18'

Prop

Footings with "U" bracket

Corner Beam Detail

Floor

Make a floor frame by toenailing four 2x8s to the corner beams, beveling the ends so that they butt up neatly against the sides of the corner beams. Add three 2x8 joists, spaced 5' on center. Add concrete blocks or stones to support the floor joists at mid-span and at the corners. Nail 2x6 tongue and groove deck boards to the floor joists, using 10d galvanized nails.

Walls

Cut and install three 2x8 rafters equally spaced between each pair of corner beams. Nail 2x6 tongue and groove "decking" horizontally across the sides of the slanted walls, mitering and beveling the ends to fit together perfectly at the corners. This can be done easily by using a compound chop saw. To provide cross ventilation, add a skylight to the back wall.

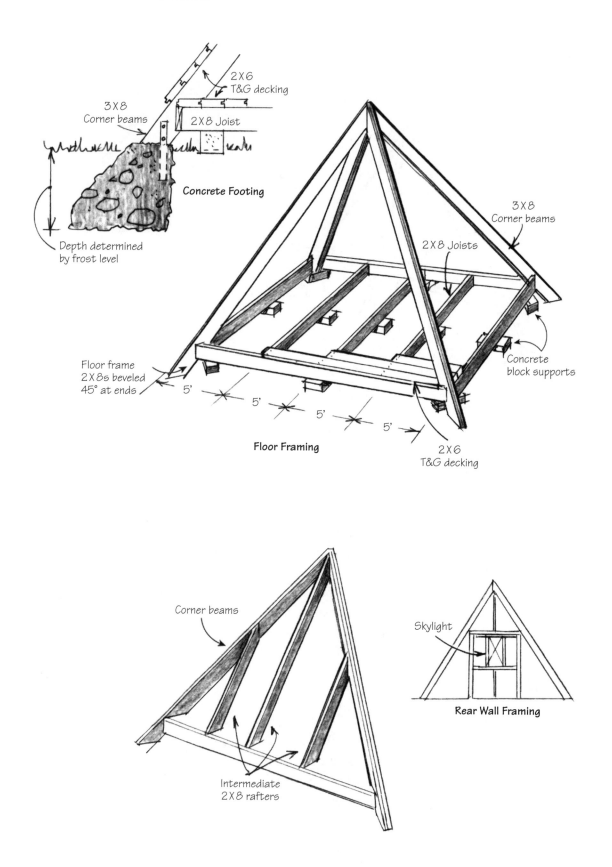

2X6
T&G decking

3X8
Corner beams

2X8 Joist

Concrete Footing

Depth determined
by frost level

2X8 Joists

3X8
Corner beams

Floor frame
2X8s beveled
45° at ends

Concrete
block supports

5'   5'   5'   5'

Floor Framing

2X6
T&G decking

Corner beams

Skylight

Intermediate
2X8 rafters

Rear Wall Framing

Door

The entrance door is a 4'x8' panel of plywood, secured by hinges. This doorway can be adapted for hot or cold weather. In the summer, 2x3 props hold up the hinged plywood panel. A 4' wide screened-in-porch can be made by attaching mosquito netting to the roof and front deck, keeping out the bugs and making an ideal place to catch summer breezes. In the winter, the panel is closed and the pyramid can be accessed through a 4' high hatch, cut out of the plywood panel and hinged on one side.

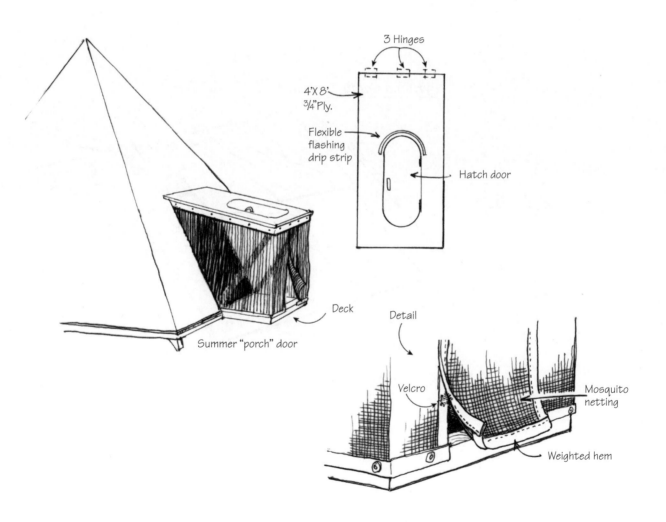

3 Hinges

4'X 8'
3/4" Ply.

Flexible flashing drip strip

Hatch door

Summer "porch" door

Deck

Detail

Velcro

Mosquito netting

Weighted hem

Roofing

There are many choices available for roofing materials, but if you are adventuresome, consider covering the entire structure with 6 mil, 54" wide reflective Mylar. First, cover the entire outside surface of the structure with 1/4" tempered hardboard (Masonite), attached using PL200 construction adhesive and 1 1/4" panel nails. Fill and sand the entire surface so it is smooth. Use a roller to apply adhesive over the hardboard and lay the Mylar strips on top of the adhesive, folding over the bottom edges of the strips and overlapping each layer by 6". Use Monel, rust-resistant staples near the bottom edges of each strip.

Pyramid Cabin Covering

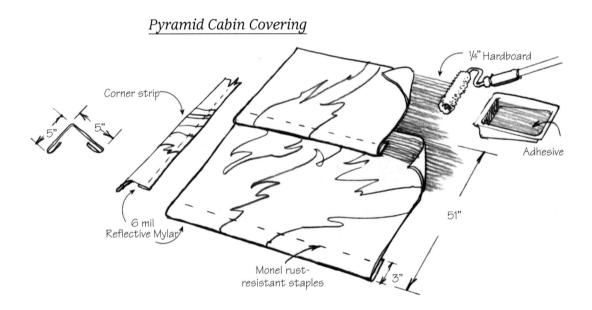

A-Frame Cabin

The A-frame cabin became very popular in the 1960s and although it went out of fashion for several years, it is worth considering as a viable building design because of its many advantages over rectangular structures. The triangular shape is stronger than a rectangular shape and the walls and roof are built as a unit requiring less lumber and less labor to build. There is also less wasted space to heat, making it more energy efficient.

One of the most important design features of the A-frame is its triangular outline, which mimics the shape of the pine trees, allowing it to look at home in a pine forest, whether in Vermont, Michigan or northern California.

Critics of the A-frame complain that the sloping walls are a disadvantage, resulting in wasted corner space and causing A-frame dwellers to unavoidably hit their heads. This problem has been solved by providing extension wings on each side, thereby improving upon the original design.

A-Frame Cabin

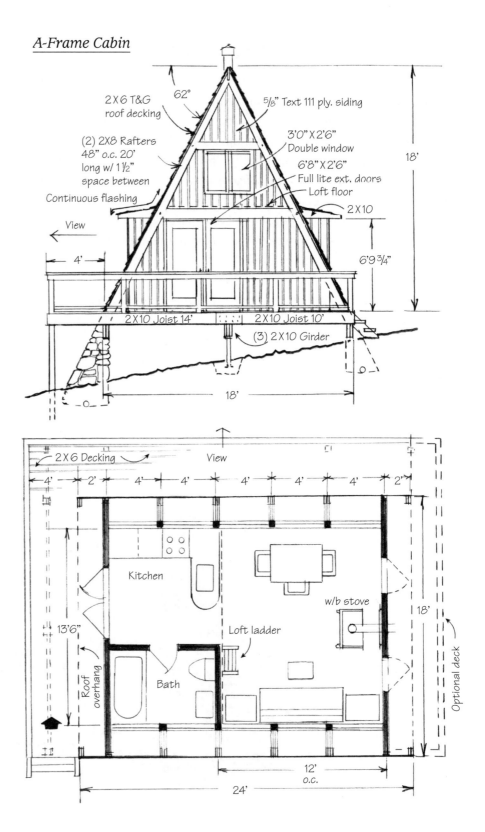

2 X 6 T&G
roof decking

62°

(2) 2X8 Rafters
48" o.c. 20'
long w/ 1 ½"
space between

Continuous flashing

5/8" Text 111 ply. siding

3'0" X 2'6"
Double window

6'8" X 2'6"
Full lite ext. doors

Loft floor

2 X 10

View

4'

18'

6'9 ¾"

2 X 10 Joist 14'   2 X 10 Joist 10'

(3) 2 X 10 Girder

18'

2 X 6 Decking   View

4'   2'   4'   4'   4'   4'   4'   2'

Kitchen

w/b stove

Loft ladder

13'6"

Roof overhang

Bath

Optional deck

18'

12'
o.c.

24'

Floor Plan

This cabin could be built by three people with average building skills in less than two months. Once the foundation and floor are in place, the remaining structure can be closed in in a matter of days.

This cabin requires many long beams that are not always available at lumber yards and difficult to transport to your building site. The solution is to order shorter lengths of lumber and nail them together at the site. Most people love to pound nails and this can be great fun for the whole family or for a group of friends if you have a "nailing party" one weekend.

Footings

Dig two 36" wide, 24' long trenches, 18" deep. To prevent frost heave in cold climates, lay a 4" diameter, perforated plastic pipe in the bottom of the trenches and run the pipes out downhill until they reach daylight (arrive above ground). Cover the bottom of the trenches with 6" of stone and fill the trench with concrete. Embed two 1/2" reinforcing rods, 6" below the surface and 12" apart.

After the concrete has cured for several days, build a 3/4" plywood backboard wall, 48" high on the inside of each trench, as shown on the next page. Make sure it is level, plumb and well braced. Build a rock foundation wall by piling rocks and cement up on the outside, filling the interior with rubble and loose stones. Slant the wall as you go up (called battering) until it reaches within 9 1/2" of the top of the plywood. Install a 24' long, double 2x10 girder flush with the plywood and level off the top with concrete.

Nailing Party

Cabin Footings

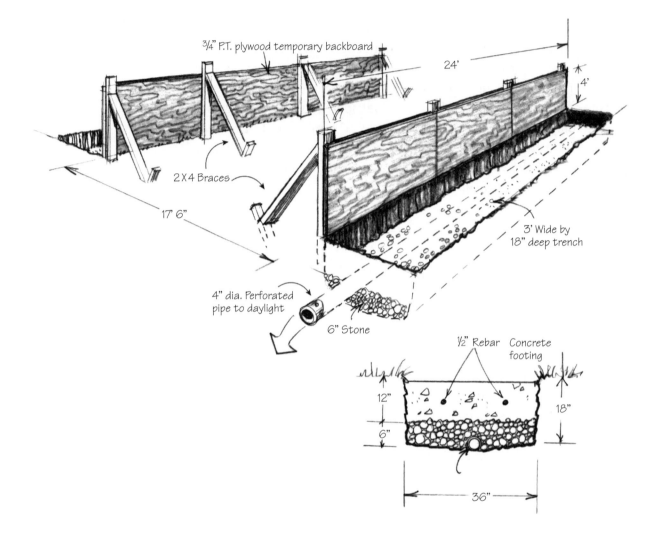

3/4" P.T. plywood temporary backboard

24'

4'

2 X 4 Braces

17' 6"

3' Wide by
18" deep trench

4" dia. Perforated
pipe to daylight

6" Stone

1/2" Rebar   Concrete
footing

12"

18"

6"

36"

Center Girder

Add a center girder by digging four 2' square holes, 8" deep, and approximately 8' apart and fill them with concrete. Before the concrete sets, stand four adjustable house jacks on top of the footing and embed bolts into the wet concrete. Adjust the house jacks so that the tops are level with the two side support girders and bolt in a 24' long center girder, made up of three 2x10 boards nailed together.

Center Girder

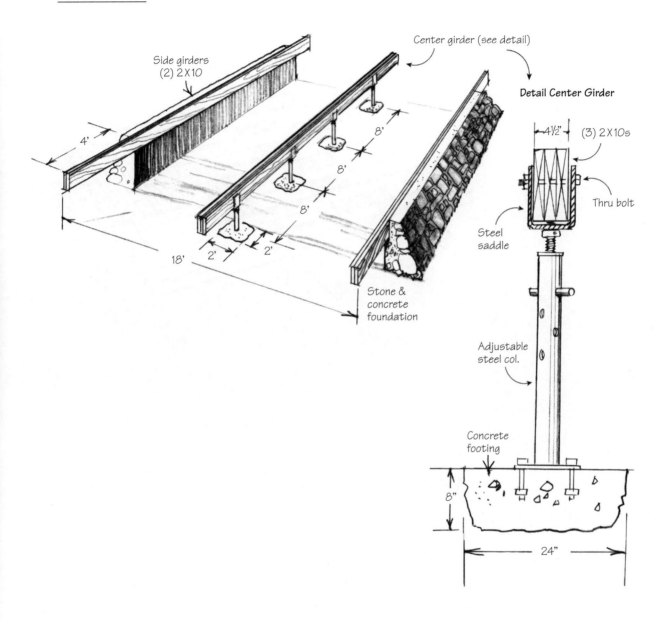

Side girders
(2) 2X10

Center girder (see detail)

Detail Center Girder

4½"

(3) 2X10s

Thru bolt

Steel
saddle

Adjustable
steel col.

Concrete
footing

8"

24"

Stone &
concrete
foundation

4'

18'

2'

2'

8'

8'

8'

Floor Framing

Build the floor joists out of 22' 2x10s, spaced 4' on center. If 22' long
lumber is unavailable, splice together one 12' and one 10' 2x10. Make
sure the joint lies over the center girder.

Floor Framing

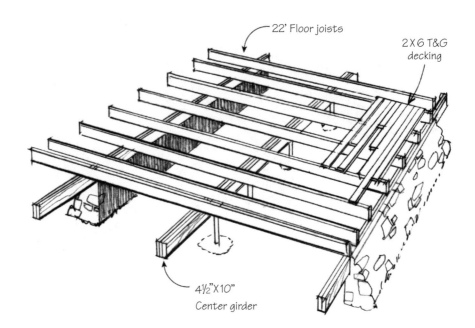

A-Frame

Assemble the A-frames flat on the deck as shown on the following page. Assemble the ridgeboard by splicing together several pieces of 1x8, to make up 24'. Raise each A-frame into position, one at a time. Note that the bottom of the A-frame legs fit neatly around the floor joists. Hold them temporarily in place with 2x4 braces, and once they are properly aligned, nail them together permanently. The ridgeboard fits into the slot provided in the top of the A-frame.

Wing Extensions

The wing extensions are built in the conventional manner, using 2x4 or 2x6 studs. Order or build your windows in advance so you know for sure what sizes to frame for.

The A-Frame

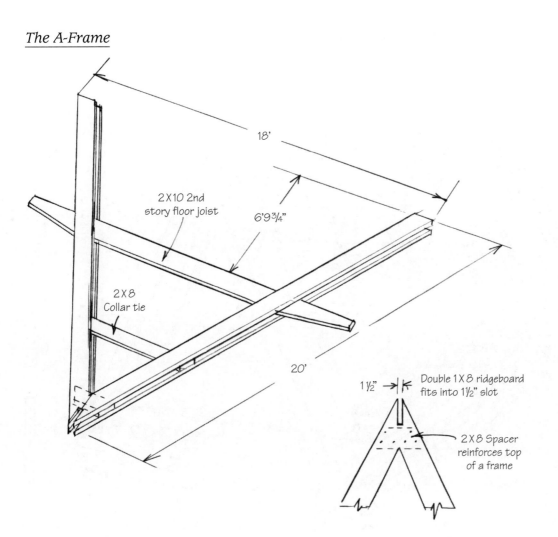

End Walls

After the roof and wing extensions are built, fill in the gabled front and rear walls, using conventional 2x4 studs or 2x6 framing. Take careful measurements of the openings and build the sections on the deck floor, then raise them up and nail them in place.

Doors and Windows

Order full lite (one full glass panel) exterior doors for the front and rear walls. Insulated glass (double pane) is required in most areas, preferably with tempered glass. There are many styles and manufacturers of windows, so take some time to compare prices, since this will be a major

A-Frame End Walls Construction

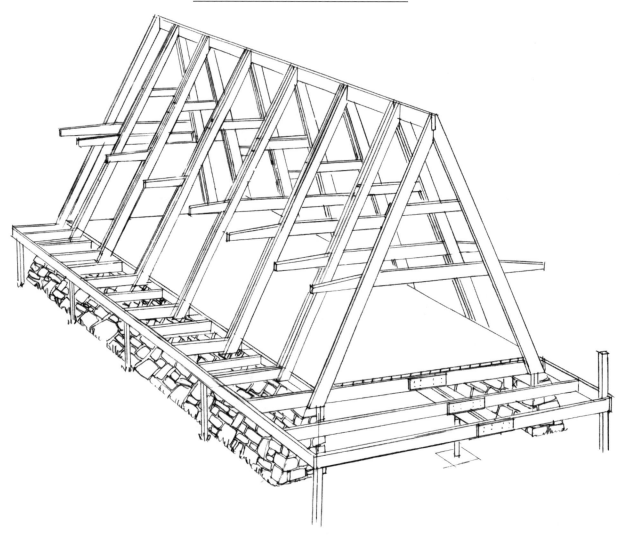

cabin expense. Bare wood windows are less expensive, but require maintenance every two or three years. If you can afford clad windows, you won't be spending your future vacations painting.

Exterior Siding

Although these plans call for plywood siding, there are many other types of siding to choose from, such as horizontal, shiplap, or tongue and groove boards.

A-Frame Cabin: Section

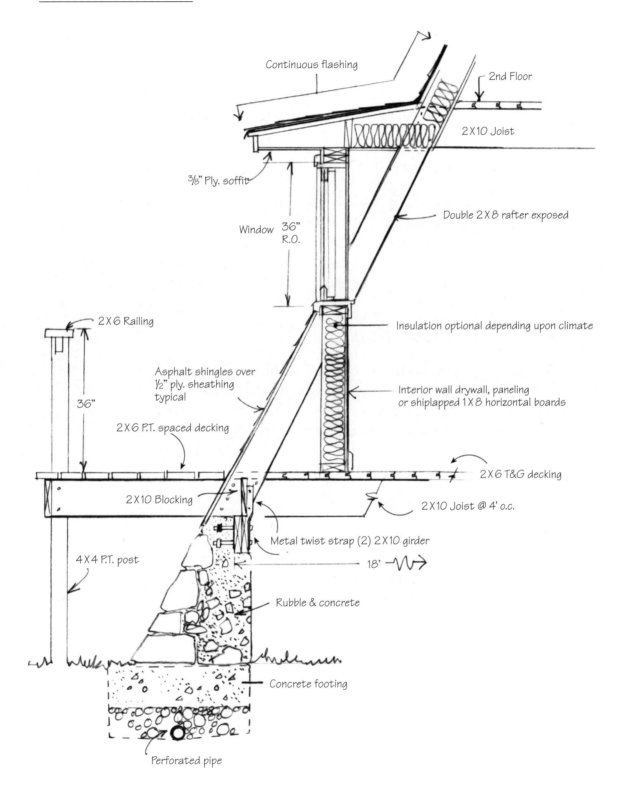

Continuous flashing

2nd Floor

2 X 10 Joist

3/8" Ply. soffit

Window 36" R.O.

Double 2 X 8 rafter exposed

2 X 6 Railing

Insulation optional depending upon climate

Asphalt shingles over 1/2" ply. sheathing typical

Interior wall drywall, paneling or shiplapped 1 X 8 horizontal boards

36"

2 X 6 P.T. spaced decking

2 X 6 T&G decking

2 X 10 Blocking

2 X 10 Joist @ 4' o.c.

Metal twist strap (2) 2 X 10 girder

18'

4 X 4 P.T. post

Rubble & concrete

Concrete footing

Perforated pipe

Roof

The roof is held together using 2x6 tongue and groove decking, making the structure extra strong. When installing these boards, the same rules apply as for the floor decking—stagger the joints and span three or more beams. Cover the roof decking with 15 lb. tar paper and your choice of asphalt or cedar shingles or shakes.

Exterior Deck

The exterior decks are framed with 2x10 joists held up by 4x4 pressure-treated posts, embedded in the ground below the frost line. Extend the posts 36" above the deck to provide support for the 2x6 railing (laid flat). Use 2x6 pressure-treated boards, allowing a 1/4" space between each board for drainage and ventilation.

Insulation

Although the underside of the roof decking is attractive, you may want to cover it with insulation by furring out between the A-frames with 2x4s or 2x6s. This, of course, depends on your climate and heating needs. You might instead consider applying rigid insulation to the exterior of the roof, allowing the decking to show from the inside.

Interior

Design the interior of your cabin according to your budget and requirements. You could have a conventional kitchen stove supplied by a propane tank stored under the cabin; this is also a perfect place to store firewood since it is well protected from the weather. A wood-burning stove or zero clearance fireplace is almost a must in this cozy cabin. Firewood for immediate use can be stored on an optional 2' deep deck just behind the fireplace or stove. Water can be supplied by an outside well and stored in a holding tank under the cabin. Check with your local board of health for septic system requirements.

A-Frame Interior

This cabin sleeps two comfortably in the loft with an occasional guest on the couch below. The many windows that surround the cabin make it a cheerful, bright place to spend the weekend, even in rainy weather.

Pole Built Cabin

Several years ago, we had occasion to deliver some drawings to an architect who was a partner in one of New York City's most prestigious architectural firms. As we drove up a remote dirt road on the end of Long Island, we expected to find an "architectural statement" reminiscent of the firm's unique architectural style. Instead, we found a simple one-room cabin built on poles, with a glass wall facing west toward Peconic Bay, to catch the evening sunsets. It wasn't too difficult to see what the owner's priorities were. The stress and fast pace of his Manhattan office were left far behind, the city noises replaced by the occasional call of a soaring osprey, searching for its evening meal. The cabin contained only the essentials. The room was dominated by a bed, which also served as a couch, and was covered with an Oriental spread

and dozens of pillows. Utilitarian items, like kitchen appliances, were built-in, leaving the main focus on the spectacular view out the front windows.

This design requires eleven #6 or #7 class poles, approximately 10' to 18' long. You may find poles at a local saw mill, or you may be able to buy second-hand utility poles. If neither of these are available in your area, substitute pressure-treated 8x8 square posts, which may have to be special ordered from your lumber yard. Pole building is a relatively inexpensive and labor-saving method of building, especially adaptable to sites that are either bordering water or on a slope. The poles should be embedded a minimum of 4' into the ground. This can best be done by hiring a contractor who specializes in pole construction. A 20' pressure-treated pole might weigh over 500 pounds and require heavy equipment and several workers to install.

If you are ambitious, and the soil in your area is not too hard, dig holes 16" in diameter, 4' to 5' deep, using a manual post hole digger and a 5' crow bar. Where we live in Long Island, the soil is mostly sandy and a 48" deep hole can easily be dug in about fifteen minutes. The same hole might take four hours in Arkansas where the soil is rocky and filled with clay.

When erecting the poles, make sure that the side facing the inside of the cabin is plumb, since the walls will be attached to the inside. Notice that all the poles are placed on the outside of the cabin (see Pole Layout) so that the cabin walls can be built independent of the poles. It also allows for some room for adjustment when attaching the main structure to the poles.

One tip that deserves repeating: it is a mistake to backfill the poles as soon as they are in place. It is better to brace the poles on three sides, using temporary boards, and backfill only when the floor and ceiling beams are in place. If you ever had to dig out an incorrectly placed pole, you will appreciate this advice.

Digging Holes and Setting Poles

Once the posts are in place, construction should proceed at a fast pace. The walls can actually be pre-built in your backyard, transported on a flatbed truck and set up at the site. The roof, which appears to be flat, is actually pitched slightly toward the rear to allow for drainage or as a catchment for rainwater if a cistern is being considered.

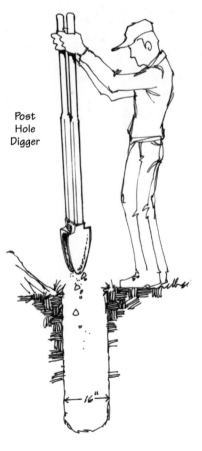

Post Hole Digger

Pole Built Cabin

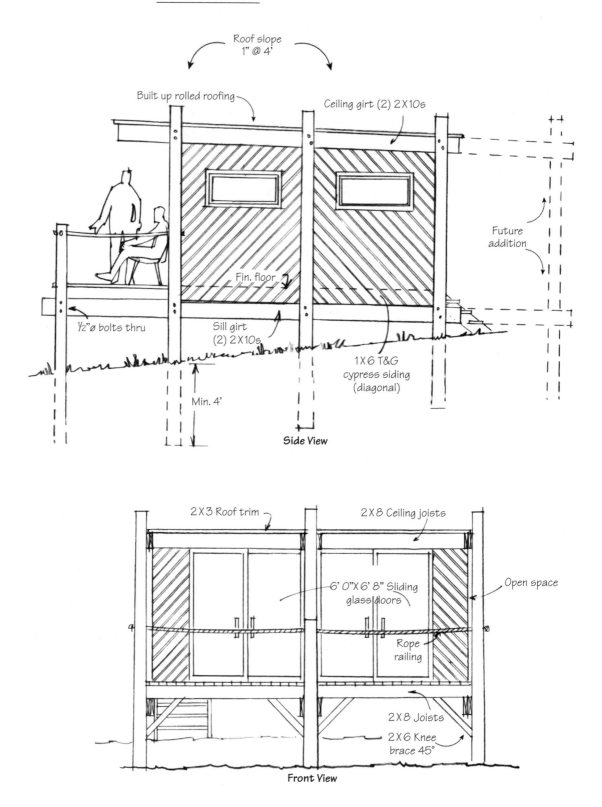

Roof slope
1" @ 4'

Built up rolled roofing

Ceiling girt (2) 2 X 10s

Fin. floor

½"ø bolts thru

Sill girt
(2) 2 X 10s

1 X 6 T&G
cypress siding
(diagonal)

Future
addition

Min. 4'

Side View

2 X 3 Roof trim

2 X 8 Ceiling joists

6' 0"X 6' 8" Sliding
glass doors

Open space

Rope
railing

2 X 8 Joists

2 X 6 Knee
brace 45°

Front View

Pole Built Cabin Floor Plan

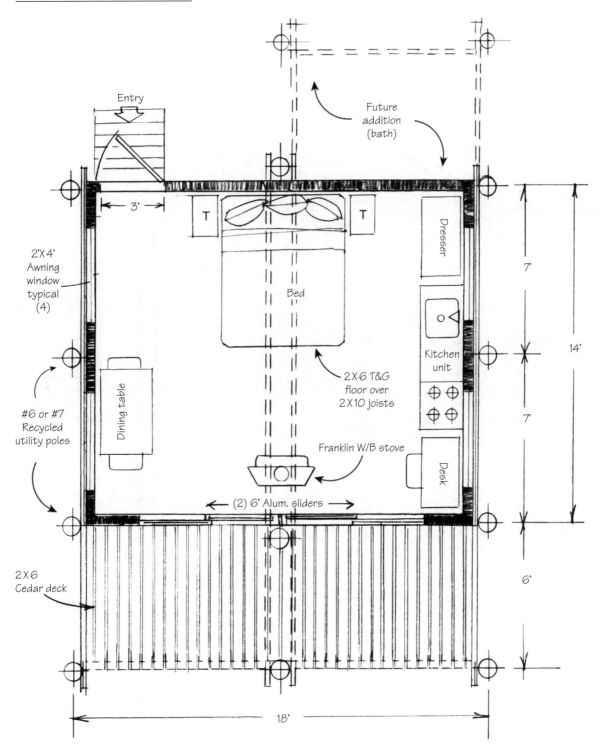

Entry

Future addition (bath)

2'X 4' Awning window typical (4)

3'

Dresser

Bed

T   T

2 X 6 T&G floor over 2 X 10 joists

Kitchen unit

#6 or #7 Recycled utility poles

Dining table

Franklin W/B stove

Desk

(2) 6' Alum. sliders

7

14'

7

2 X 6 Cedar deck

6'

18'

Pole Built Cabin Construction

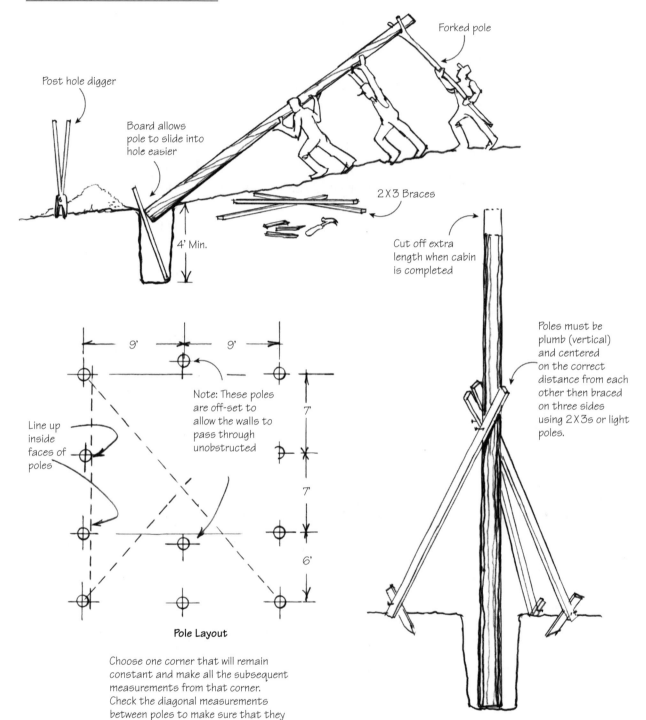

Post hole digger

Forked pole

Board allows
pole to slide into
hole easier

4' Min.

2 X 3 Braces

Cut off extra
length when cabin
is completed

Poles must be
plumb (vertical)
and centered
on the correct
distance from each
other then braced
on three sides
using 2 X 3s or light
poles.

9'   9'

Note: These poles
are off-set to
allow the walls to
pass through
unobstructed

7'

7'

6'

Line up
inside
faces of
poles

Pole Layout

Choose one corner that will remain
constant and make all the subsequent
measurements from that corner.
Check the diagonal measurements
between poles to make sure that they
are equal.

Pole Built Cabin Construction Detail

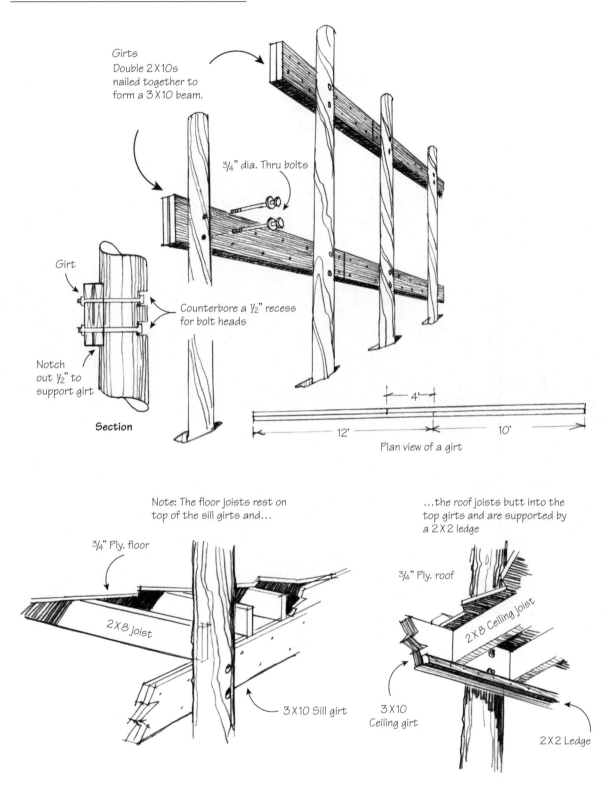

Girts
Double 2X10s
nailed together to
form a 3X10 beam.

¾" dia. Thru bolts

Girt

Counterbore a ½" recess
for bolt heads

Notch
out ½" to
support girt

Section

4'

12'   10'

Plan view of a girt

Note: The floor joists rest on
top of the sill girts and...

¾" Ply. floor

2X8 joist

3X10 Sill girt

...the roof joists butt into the
top girts and are supported by
a 2X2 ledge

¾" Ply. roof

2X8 Ceiling joist

3X10
Ceiling girt

2X2 Ledge

Pole Built Cabin Construction

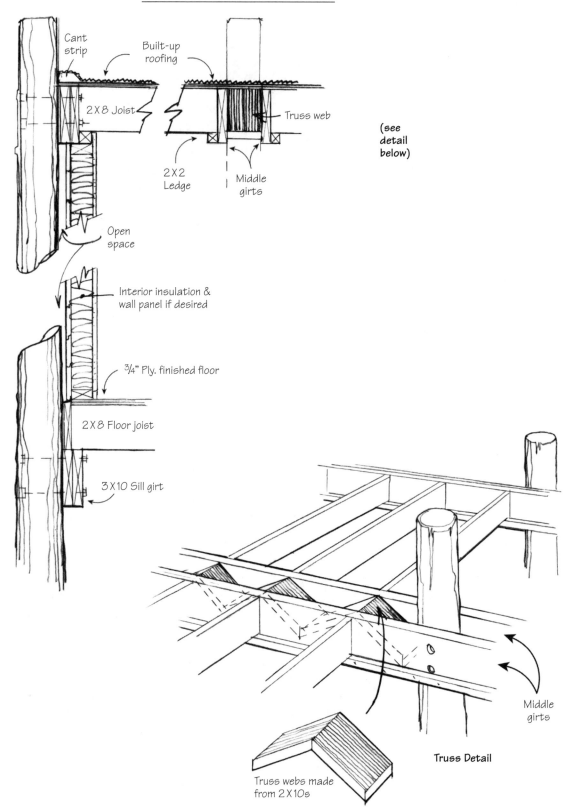

Cant strip

Built-up roofing

2 X 8 Joist

Truss web

(see detail below)

2 X 2 Ledge

Middle girts

Open space

Interior insulation & wall panel if desired

¾" Ply. finished floor

2 X 8 Floor joist

3 X 10 Sill girt

Middle girts

Truss webs made from 2 X 10s

Truss Detail

The floor and ceiling girts running front to back are made up of double pieces of 2x10s, nailed together to form a 3x10 beam. Stagger the joints so they are 4' apart.

Note: The floor joists lay on top of the 2x10 floor girts; however, the ceiling rafters butt up to the top girts and are supported by a 2x2 ledge so that the tops of the rafters and the girts are flush. This decreases the overall height of the building.

It is important to stiffen the two center girts by forming a makeshift truss out of scrap lumber (see Truss Detail). Once the cabin is framed, add 2x6 diagonal knee braces to the posts to stiffen the structure against heavy wind loads (see Front elevation).

Timber-Framed Guest Cabin

When a cabin is just not big enough to accommodate an expanding family or weekend friends, a guest cabin can be the perfect solution. Plumbing is not essential because the guests can use the facilities in the main cabin. A simple guest cabin can be built with only the basic requirements of shelter and privacy in mind. The only furniture that is necessary is a couple of beds and two dressers for clothes storage. We have included a covered front porch in the design, which makes a relaxing place to sit while waiting for hosts or parents in the main cabin to wake up and brew coffee. On chilly evenings, the cabin can be warmed with a portable electric or propane heater. Extra blankets can be stored at the foot of each bed in handmade chests.

This is a nice cabin to make out of 4x6 cedar beams, using timber framing for the main structure and 2x4s to support the siding. Screens should be put on the windows and shutters add an accent, as well as provide security when the cabin is closed up for the winter. The curve to the roof gives the cabin a snug feeling and makes it

look almost thatched. The curved top edge of the rafters can be easily cut, using an electric jig saw. Simply start out with slightly larger (2x8 instead of 2x6) boards. These cuts can be done in less than an hour and will give the cabin a very distinctive look. Cedar or asphalt shingles will bend over the curve of the spaced 1x4 sheathing which covers the rafters.

Guest Cabin

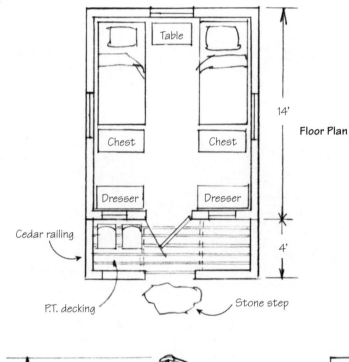

Floor Plan

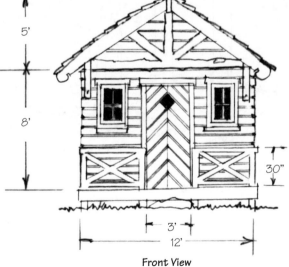

Front View

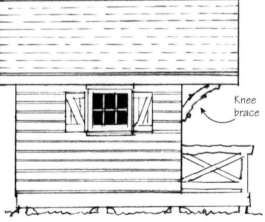

Side View

Make the knee braces, which support the roof of the exterior porch, out of curved branches from trees found in the woods. The front porch can be trimmed with peeled cedar branches to give the cabin a truly rustic look. Using the same siding on the guest cabin that is on the main cabin, will make it appear to be a mini-version of the parent cabin.

This simple cabin should be fun to build and can easily be accomplished by one person in less than a month.

Construction Details

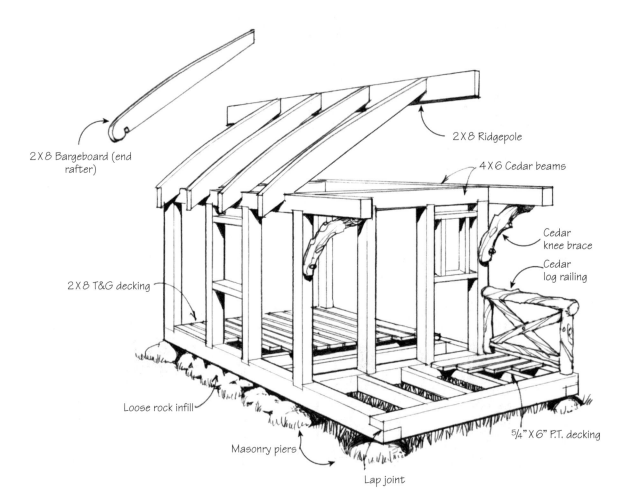

2 X 8 Bargeboard (end rafter)

2 X 8 Ridgepole

4 X 6 Cedar beams

Cedar knee brace

Cedar log railing

2 X 8 T&G decking

Loose rock infill

Masonry piers

Lap joint

5/4" X 6" P.T. decking

Photo: Skip Hine

Richard & Joan Bartlett's addition onto a 1940 log cabin, Richmond, Mass.

RuAnn Ewing's cabin in War Eagle, Arkansas.

Wallis Lawrence's writing cabin in Woodstock, N.Y.

Connie McDermott's cabin, made from chestnut logs. Wolf Lake, Catskills, New York.

Connie McDermott's cabin porch.

MacEagle's winter cabin near Middlebury, Vermont.

Mark & Wendy Dwires' year-round cabin, near Middlebury, Vermont.

The Dwire workshop cabin.

Ken and RuAnn Ewing's cabin interior, Hindsville, Arkansas.

Phil Berg's bunkhouse cabin, East Hampton, N.Y.

Nancy Fitzpatrick & Lincoln Russell's cabin near Stockbridge, Mass.

Historic 1753 cabin reconstructed in Williamstown, Mass.

Log cabin on stone foundation near Middlebury, Vermont.

Preston Phillips' architect's studio in Bridgehampton, N.Y.

Photo: John Hulsey

Cabin built by artists Ann Trusty and John Hulsey, in Lawrence, Kansas.

Photo: Ellsworth Rundlett

Ellsworth Rundlett's cabin in Frenchboro, Maine.

Ray Sherman and Lennie Golay's Adirondack cabin.

Tuck Gaisford in front of his log cabin, New York state.

Caribbean cabin, French West Indies.

"Eagle's Nest"—Foster MacEdward's mountaintop cabin near Middlebury, Vermont.

David Hense's cabin in Olympia, Washington.

Don Metz, architect, built his log cabin deep in the New Hampshire woods.

Cabin built by Docie Woodard & Linda Beal, Everett, WA.

Authors' weekend retreat, fifty miles from New York City.

Simone Manheim's guest cabin overlooking the Atlantic Ocean, East Hampton, N.Y.

Lakeside Cabin

This lakeside cabin accommodates a family of four comfortably while allowing for expansion should a fifth member arrive. It features a large 16'x16' open room for combined living and dining, with French doors that open out onto a screened-in porch, with a view of the lake. The porch makes a wonderful place to sleep, drifting off to the night sounds of katydids, frogs and loons while being protected from mosquitoes.

Lakeside Cabin Floor Plans

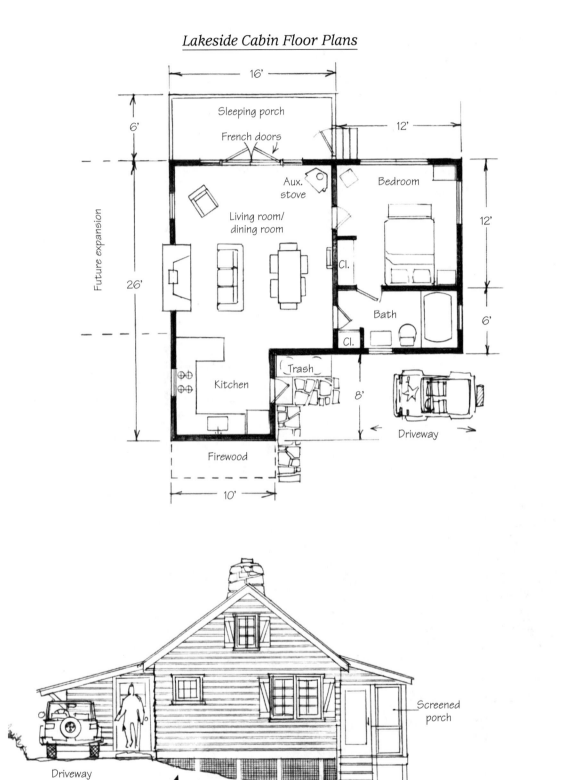

16'

6'

Sleeping porch

French doors

12'

Aux. stove

Bedroom

Future expansion

Living room/ dining room

12'

26'

Cl.

Cl.

Bath

6'

Trash

8'

Kitchen

Driveway

Firewood

10'

Driveway

Screened porch

4'

Piers @ 4' o.c.

Lattice

On another side of the living/dining room is a master bedroom with a sleeping loft above it. This cabin can be built using standard 2x4 or 2x6 construction. It can be left unfinished on the inside or insulated and paneled, depending on the climate and the cabin builder's budget. Storage for trash and firewood are conveniently located right outside the kitchen door.

The ceiling height of the first floor is kept purposely low to allow more space for the overhead sleeping loft, while still complying with the building code requirements of 7' 3". This also gives the overall building a lower profile, consistent with most cabin designs.

Lakeside Cabin Sections

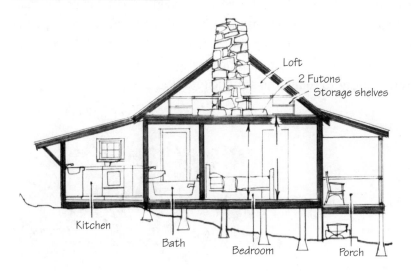

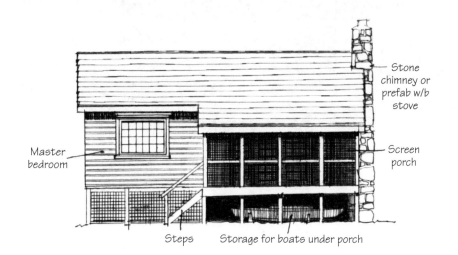

Japanese Moongazing Cabin

The design of this Japanese moongazing cabin was influenced by the Japanese bath houses and the Shinto shrines in Kyoto and surrounding areas. It has all the essentials for a weekend cabin while maintaining an aura of simplicity. The one 12'x16' open room contains a kitchen, storage areas, and space to put two futons for sleeping. Sliding doors at the back side of the cabin open to reveal a hot tub which becomes an integral part of the "engawa," or Japanese verandah that surrounds the house. Toilet facilities are separate from the house. This cabin is an ideal weekend retreat, guest house or backyard spa, a haven to escape from an otherwise hectic life and a refuge for reading and meditation, practicing Tai Chi, and soaking in a hot tub while drinking green tea. The simple design should emanate a mood of peacefulness and relaxation. Furnishings should be kept to a minimum in order to retain the simplicity of the design.

This cabin, built using post and beam construction, incorporates intricate joints at several of the connections. The framework could all be built on the ground in advance and erected by three or four people, similar to a barn raising. A less ambitious and easier method of building is to frame the cabin using standard "two-by" lumber, however, this will not be as true to the Japanese building traditions. The sliding doors are made of translucent acrylic sheeting, framed with strips of redwood and covered with a redwood grill, giving it the look of a Japanese shoji screen. The 2x6 decking should be built out of tongue and groove clear cedar or redwood, depending on your budget. The roof is made from hand-split cedar shakes, which will weather to a soft grey in time.

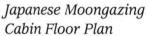

Japanese Moongazing Cabin Floor Plan

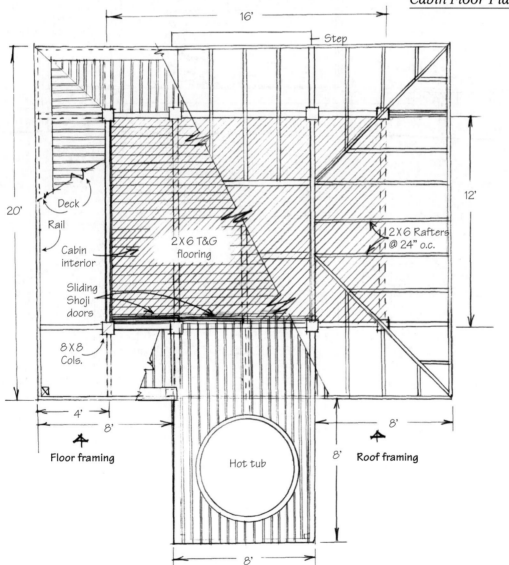

16'

Step

20'

Deck

Rail

Cabin interior

2X6 T&G flooring

12'

2X6 Rafters @ 24" o.c.

Sliding Shoji doors

8X8 Cols.

4'

8'

Floor framing

Hot tub

8'

8'

8'

Roof framing

Japanese Moongazing Cabin Sections

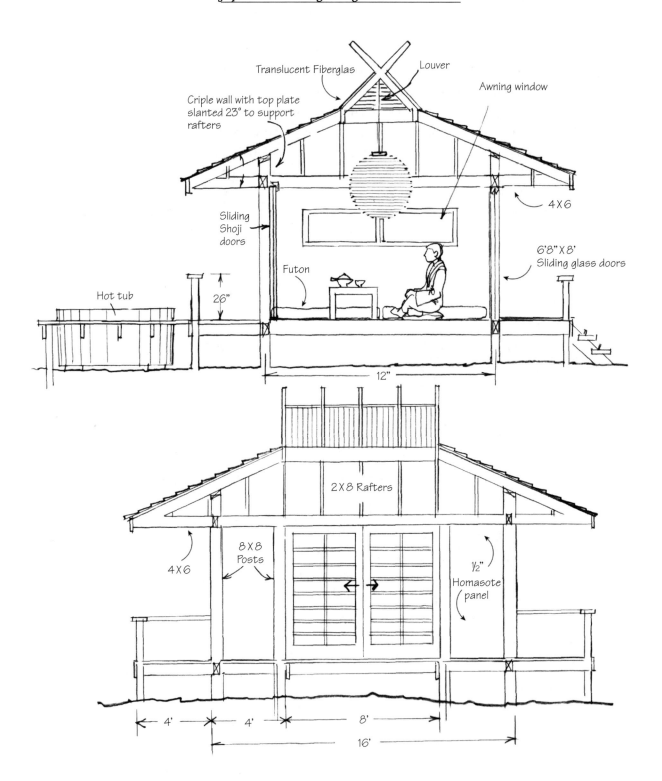

Translucent Fiberglas

Louver

Awning window

Criple wall with top plate slanted 23° to support rafters

4 X 6

Sliding Shoji doors

6'8" X 8' Sliding glass doors

Futon

Hot tub

26"

12"

2 X 8 Rafters

4 X 6

8 X 8 Posts

½" Homasote panel

4'   4'   8'

16'

Japanese Moongazing Cabin Framing

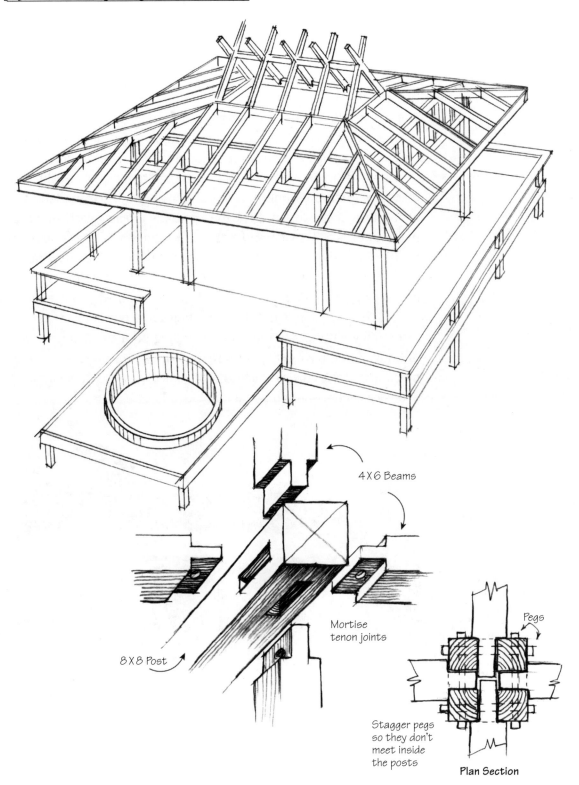

4 X 6 Beams

Mortise
tenon joints

8 X 8 Post

Pegs

Stagger pegs
so they don't
meet inside
the posts

Plan Section

Mediterranean Cabin

Our quest for cabins has taken us many places, the most romantic and remote being the island of Elba, Italy, where our friends Ernesto and Rosabianca spend their summers living in a cabin carved out of the side of a hill, overlooking the Mediterranean Sea. For them, this one-room (plus bath) summer cabin is a natural extension of the camper which they vacationed in for many years in Marina di Campo. The cabin is built out of concrete, colored to match the ground around it and blends in perfectly with the surrounding rocky cliffs. Although the cabin measures only 24' wide by 12' deep, it can sleep five people in a pinch. Designed like the interior of a sailing yacht, it makes maximum use of space and has two trundle beds that double as couches. The sliding glass doors open to a terrace with a breathtaking view of stars above, the harbor of Porto Azzurro below and the twinkling lights of Capoliveri in the distance, perched on an adjacent mountain. Our friends usually slide their table out onto the terrace where they eat most of their meals, grilling on a small electric grill. Although they have electricity, many similar residences use only propane for their utilities. Each 8 gallon tank of gas lasts about a month and is easily transported by hand.

Cut & Fill Excavation

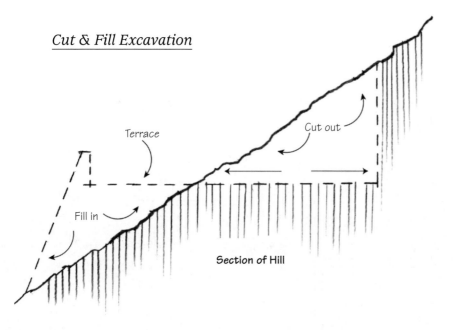

Terrace

Cut out

Fill in

Section of Hill

Building this cabin is similar to building a concrete block foundation for a standard house. You may want to bring in professional masons to do this part, or, if you feel ambitious, you can build it yourself. Begin by excavating a 12'x24' area. Pitch the dirt and rocks forward to build up a level area on which to build the terrace.

To make the footings for the cabin, dig a trench 2' wide and 8" deep around the perimeter of the excavated area. Pour a concrete footing, 16" wide and 8" deep, with two lengths of 1/2" rebar running through it. Use a 2x8 board as a form to hold the wet concrete. Install a 4" diameter perforated drain pipe, sloped 1/4" per foot toward the front of the site. Fill the trench with coarse stone.

Build the walls out of 8" thick concrete blocks and mortar. Pour a 4" thick concrete floor and outside deck, using 6"x6" wire mesh, as reinforcement. Allow for a 4" drop between the inside floor and the outside patio to prevent rain from flooding in. Hopefully, you will have a convenient way to bring the gas-powered concrete mixer and a truckload of sand, gravel and cement to the site.

Concrete takes one day to harden to the touch and can actually be drilled or cut when it is at this "green" stage. It reaches its approximate final strength in 28 days, but you can build on it after it has set for only three days. Spray the concrete with water and cover it with plastic to keep in the moisture while it is curing.

Pilasters or interior columns cast into the walls may be necessary, especially in the rear wall, to resist the pressure from the outside

Mediterranean Cabin Floor Plans & Foundation

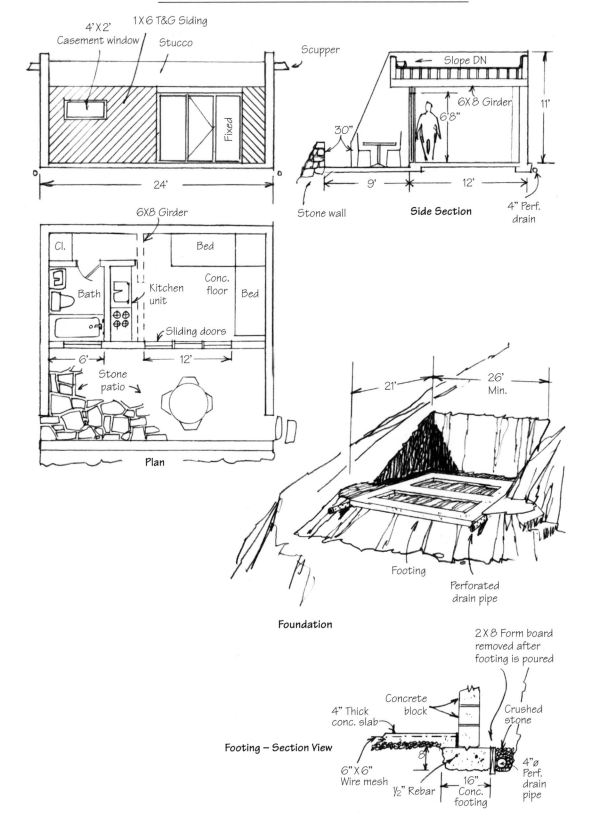

4' X 2'
Casement window

1 X 6 T&G Siding

Stucco

Scupper

Fixed

24'

Slope DN

6 X 8 Girder

6'8"

11'

30"

9'

12'

Stone wall

Side Section

4" Perf.
drain

6 X 8 Girder

Cl.

Bath

Bed

Conc.
floor

Bed

Kitchen
unit

Sliding doors

6'

12'

Stone
patio

Plan

21'

26'
Min.

Footing

Perforated
drain pipe

Foundation

2 X 8 Form board
removed after
footing is poured

Concrete
block

4" Thick
conc. slab

Crushed
stone

Footing – Section View

8"

6" X 6"
Wire mesh

½" Rebar

16"
Conc.
footing

4"ø
Perf.
drain
pipe

earth. Consult an engineer in your area for local regulations and codes. Lay a sheet of heavy plastic under the floor slab before you start pouring, to prevent future moisture from wicking up through the concrete.

When building the walls, provide pockets for the ceiling joists to rest in. The joists will not only support the roof, but will also help prevent the walls from caving in towards the interior. Use 2x10s, spaced 12" on center, and supported near the middle of the 24' span by a built-up 6x8 girder running from the back to the front of the cabin.

Cover the roof with 3/4" exterior plywood, sloped slightly to the front, to provide a run off for the rainwater. If you are using a cistern to collect rainwater, cover the plywood roof with galvanized sheet metal and provide scuppers on the sides to direct the water down. Otherwise, use three layers of tar saturated 15 lb. felt, nailed over sheathing paper, and cover with gravel.

Build the front wall of the cabin using standard lumber, installing three sliding glass doors which open onto a terrace.

Before backfilling the side and rear walls, waterproof the concrete blocks by coating them with black asphalt. If you will be using the cabin in the winter, cover the walls with 2" (blue) Styrofoam rigid insulation. Cover the Styrofoam with sheets of expanded metal and three coats of stucco/cement.

Cabin Reflections

If the call of the outdoors rings loudly for you, why not take the first blow at civilization's shackles while senses are keen and muscles vigorous? Why not make the first move now, even if it is only to acquire a retreat in nearby woods.
– Henry David Thoreau

OUTFITTING A CABIN

W̶e use our cabin as a weekend retreat to connect ourselves to the world
of nature. From the balcony of our little porch we can see bass jumping
in the pond, deer grazing in the adjoining meadow and Canada geese flying
overhead. Our days are spent hiking trails overlooking the Hudson River, and
our evenings are spent cooking meals over the wood-burning stove and listening
to crickets and bull frogs as we fall asleep.

—Jeanie Stiles

Cabin Furniture

Before going out and spending a lot of money on cabin furniture, consider building some of it yourself. Even if you didn't build your cabin, you may find building cabin furniture well within your capabilities, especially if you prefer the rustic look which requires less critical workmanship and no time-consuming finishing.

When rustic furniture is mentioned, people often think of the great Adirondack camps with their gnarled, wood tables and chairs made from twisted pieces of hickory and bent willow branches. There are several excellent books on building this furniture, most notably Daniel Mack's *Making Rustic Furniture* and Ralph Kylloe's *Rustic Style*, to mention a few. The building of rustic furniture has become more popular in the last decade, partially because of the boom in log homes. The work of craftsmen and craftswomen can be seen in stores all over the country, and even large companies have begun mass producing and selling rustic furniture through catalogs.

In the following section, we describe and illustrate the basic tools for building rustic furniture and some practical furniture designs, most of which can easily be made out of materials found in the woods.

First of all you will need a good collection of tools. A bow saw which cuts easily through stubborn wet wood. It comes in several sizes and with different teeth for cutting everything from small branches to large logs. A heavy-duty rasp (file) used for shaping wood quickly—not for smoothing surfaces. A wooden mallet for knocking joints together without damaging the wood. A sharp 1/2" chisel. A hatchet or broad ax for lopping off branches and rough shaping logs. A drawknife for skinning bark from logs and branches. A good brace and expansion bit for drilling different sized holes. An electric drill for drilling holes, or, with a screwdriver bit, for putting in screws. A utility knife for everything from fine whittling to rounding off the end of logs. If you are working outdoors, mark all your tools with fluorescent colored tape so they won't get lost.

Building Aids

SAWBUCK

Your back will appreciate this sawbuck. By adding four extra cross pieces in the middle of the sawbuck, the wood being sawed is supported adequately while you are cutting through it. As a result, it doesn't close and pinch the saw blade.

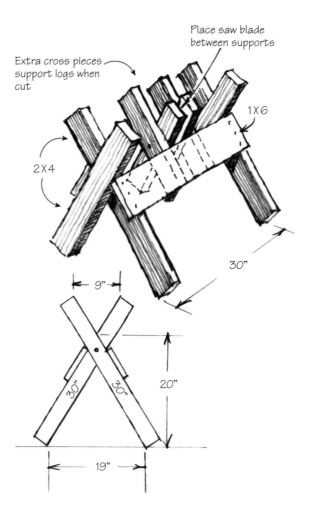

WORK TABLE

If you need a flat work area, this table is easy and inexpensive to make. Made from one piece of 3/4" plywood, it can be folded up and easily stored when not in use. The height can be changed by adjusting the length of the ropes.

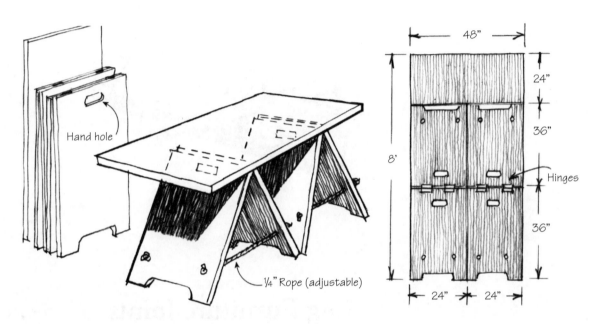

LOG PEELER BRACKET

Removing the bark from logs and branches can be difficult if you don't have a way of holding the log still while you are working on it. One solution is to make two "V" notched brackets. Notice that the second bracket is inverted to hold the end of the log not being worked on. Use a drawknife and "V" brackets for peeling logs.

SAW GUIDE

This device, made from two pieces of 1x4 temporarily nailed to a log, is useful for accurately cutting logs at right angles.

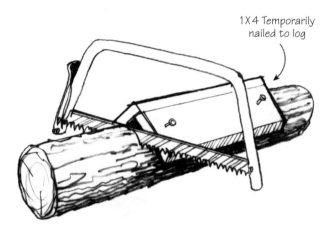

1 X 4 Temporarily nailed to log

Log Furniture Joints

How well you make the joints in your rustic furniture will determine how successful the piece is and how long it will last. Never put an unseasoned piece of wood into a seasoned piece of wood—instead, do just the opposite. Unseasoned wood will invariably shrink in time and loosen in the joint.

Peg'n Hole Joint

To cut a tenon by hand, first cut the shoulder using a small hand saw, then chip out the tenon with a chisel, and round it off using a rasp. This takes about ten minutes.

An expansion bit held in a brace can be adjusted to make any size hole, up to 2" to receive the tenon. A hole saw can cut a tenon quickly. Fill the pilot hole with glue and a 1/4" diameter peg.

Log Furniture Joints

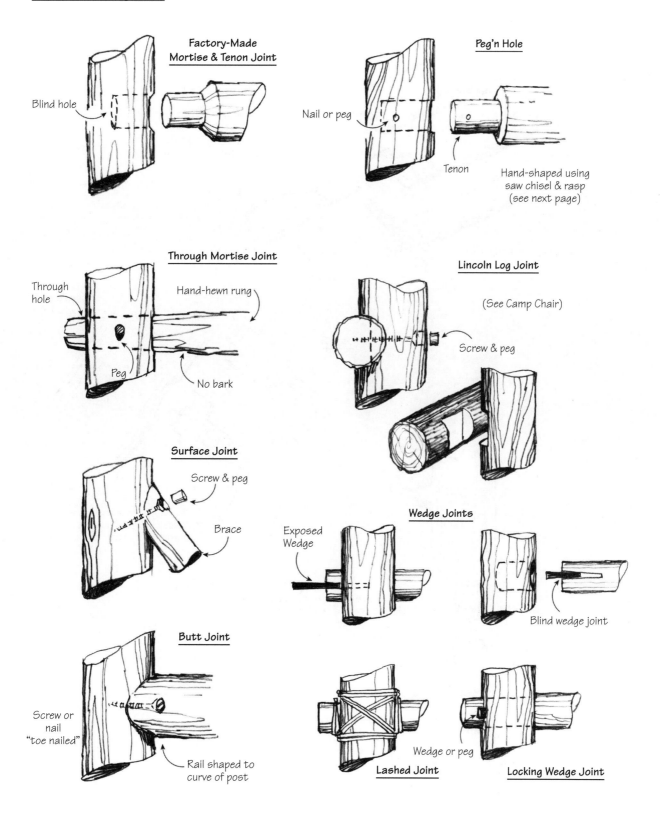

Factory-Made Mortise & Tenon Joint

Blind hole

Peg'n Hole

Nail or peg

Tenon

Hand-shaped using saw chisel & rasp (see next page)

Through Mortise Joint

Through hole

Hand-hewn rung

Peg

No bark

Lincoln Log Joint

(See Camp Chair)

Screw & peg

Surface Joint

Screw & peg

Brace

Wedge Joints

Exposed Wedge

Blind wedge joint

Butt Joint

Screw or nail "toe nailed"

Rail shaped to curve of post

Lashed Joint

Wedge or peg

Locking Wedge Joint

Peg'n Hole Joint

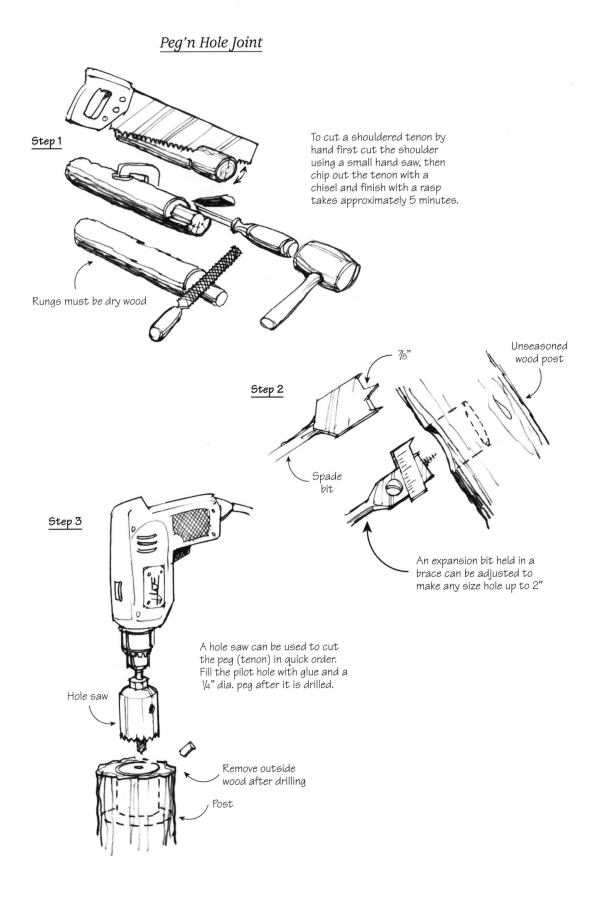

Step 1

To cut a shouldered tenon by hand first cut the shoulder using a small hand saw, then chip out the tenon with a chisel and finish with a rasp takes approximately 5 minutes.

Rungs must be dry wood

⅞"

Unseasoned wood post

Step 2

Spade bit

An expansion bit held in a brace can be adjusted to make any size hole up to 2"

Step 3

A hole saw can be used to cut the peg (tenon) in quick order. Fill the pilot hole with glue and a ¼" dia. peg after it is drilled.

Hole saw

Remove outside wood after drilling

Post

Two Simple Shelves

No cabin is complete without a few shelves filled with good reading material. An overhead shelf makes a good place to store books and a lamp. Build the shelf high enough so that the light is directed over your shoulder and onto your reading material rather than in your face.

CORNER SHELF

This simple corner shelf can be made quickly from one piece of birch wood. Cut off a 1" thick section from a log approximately 12" in diameter. Cut the section into three pieces, as shown in the diagram. Note: One bracket is cut slightly larger and overlaps the other one. Use 1 1/2" galvanized finishing nails to fasten the two brackets together at a right angle. Nail the top shelf to the brackets. Screw the brackets to the walls. This shelf is a perfect size for a small lantern, a candle or a pot of hanging ivy.

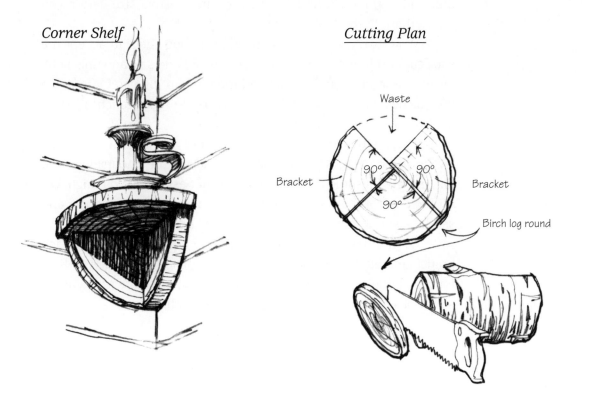

Corner Shelf

Cutting Plan

Waste

Bracket   90°   90°   Bracket

90°

Birch log round

RUSTIC LOG SHELF

Another small shelf that is rustic looking and easy to construct can be made from materials found in the woods or taken from your wood pile. Choose an interesting looking piece of wood, with straight grain and no knots, and cut off a piece approximately 20" long. Make a slab by splitting the log, using an ax or a wedge and maul. Use a bow saw to trim off the ends neatly. Whether you leave the bark on or not depends on the type of wood you are using. Prop the slab on a support branch to prevent it from rolling over and, using a chain saw, mill the top surface until it is flat. Hold the saw blade diagonally to the length of the log, fanning it back and forth.

Keep the chain saw moving diagonally across the face of the log. Never let the saw blade rest on one spot, or it will make deep cuts that are hard to remove. To get rid of the chain saw marks, use a plane to smooth the surface and make it level.

Make two shelf supports out of forked branches. It should only take a few minutes to find two perfect branches in the woods. Cut them off extra long and trim them to the finished size before you attach them to the shelf.

Make two notches in the back of the log shelf, to accept the shelf support branches. Start the cuts with a hand saw and finish hollowing them out with a chisel and then a rasp. Be careful to make the notches slightly smaller than the diameter of the branches so that the branches will fit snugly into the notches.

Squeeze the branches into the notches and screw them to the log from the back. Nail the smaller branch to the underside of the log, using a finishing nail. Although it is not essential, you might cut off the ends of the shelf support branches at a 45-degree angle and sand the surface smooth, to show off the end grain of the wood.

Counterbore a 1/4" deep hole in the top and bottom of each branch and attach the shelf to the wall, using long screws. As a final touch, whittle some short plugs ("bungs"), to fit into the screw holes, so it looks as if the shelf is held to the wall with pegs.

Rustic Log Shelf

Start with a log that is extra long and trim it to size with a bow saw

Building a Rustic Log Shelf

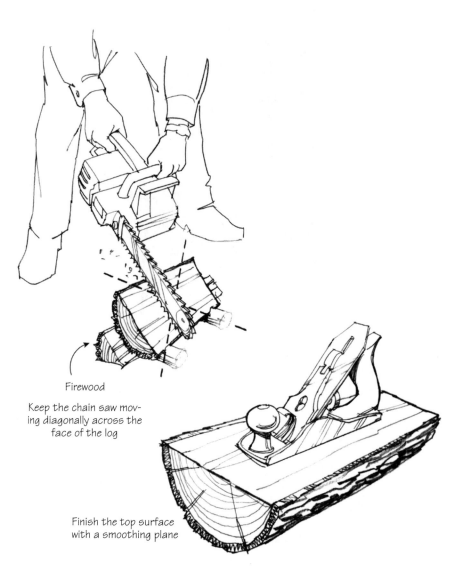

Firewood

Keep the chain saw moving diagonally across the face of the log

Finish the top surface with a smoothing plane

Building a Rustic Log Shelf

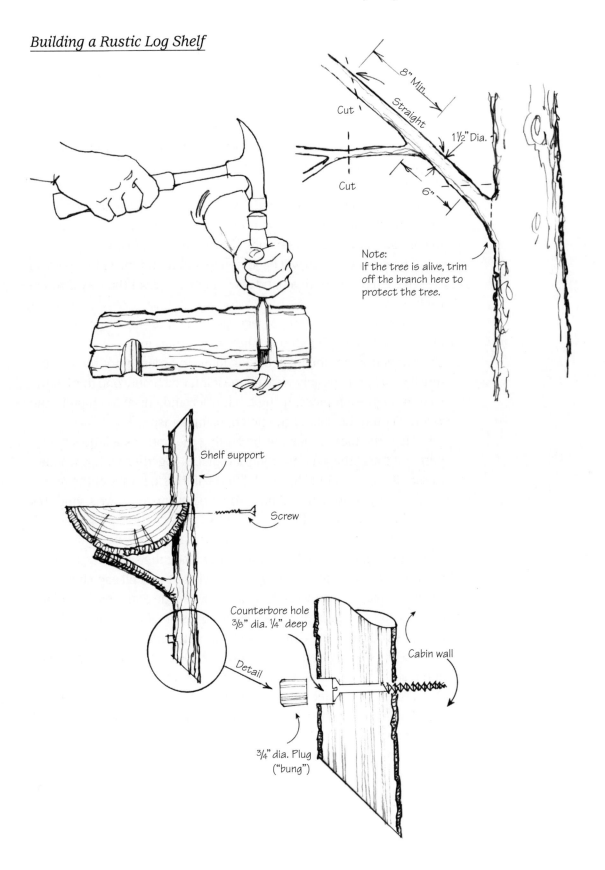

8" Min.

Cut

Straight

1½" Dia.

Cut

6"

Note:
If the tree is alive, trim
off the branch here to
protect the tree.

Shelf support

Screw

Counterbore hole
3/8" dia. ¼" deep

Cabin wall

Detail

3/4" dia. Plug
("bung")

Camp Chair

This chair is easy to make, surprisingly strong, and can be built between breakfast and lunch. The only tools you need are a tape measure, saw, chisel, hammer, rasp and screwdriver. The chair is made from two 10' long cedar poles (found at most landscape supply yards), each measuring approximately 3" at the butt and 2" at the top.

Cut the legs to the lengths shown on the plans using a hand saw. Lay the two pairs of logs on the ground and adjust the lengths to correspond to the dimensions shown on the plans. With a pencil, mark where the pieces will be joined together and make two parallel cuts in each piece. With a hand saw, cut one third of the way through each piece.

Notice that both sets of legs have a shorter leg on the outside. Make sure to take this into account when marking your joints. This chair uses the modified Lincoln log joint. In order to not remove too much wood and possibly weaken the joint, notch only one third of the way through each piece, using a hammer and chisel to chip out the wood. Flatten the seat of the notch, using a rasp.

Join the pieces together by cutting the notches a little shy of a perfect fit and then hammering the pieces together with a wooden mallet. If they don't fit, shave off a little of the side walls of the notches until they fit together tightly. You'll be surprised how strong this joint is without using glue or nails.

To hold the pieces together permanently, screw two galvanized deck screws into each joint. If you want to hide the screwheads, counterbore holes 1/4" deep, sink your screwheads and fill each hole with a wooden plug. This makes the chair look like the entire piece is made out of wood. If you think this is cheating, use real wood pegs instead of screws. Drill holes, using a 3/8" diameter spade drill bit and fill them with 3/8" diameter pegs. Always make a hole in a scrap piece and test the peg before drilling into the good piece.

Three cross pieces, called stretchers, join the two pairs of legs together. They can be slightly smaller in diameter than the legs and are notched in the same way. Make sure that the flat seats of the cross joints line up perfectly with the joints on both pairs of legs. The best way to do this is to cut and chisel the joints a little at a time,

Camp Chair

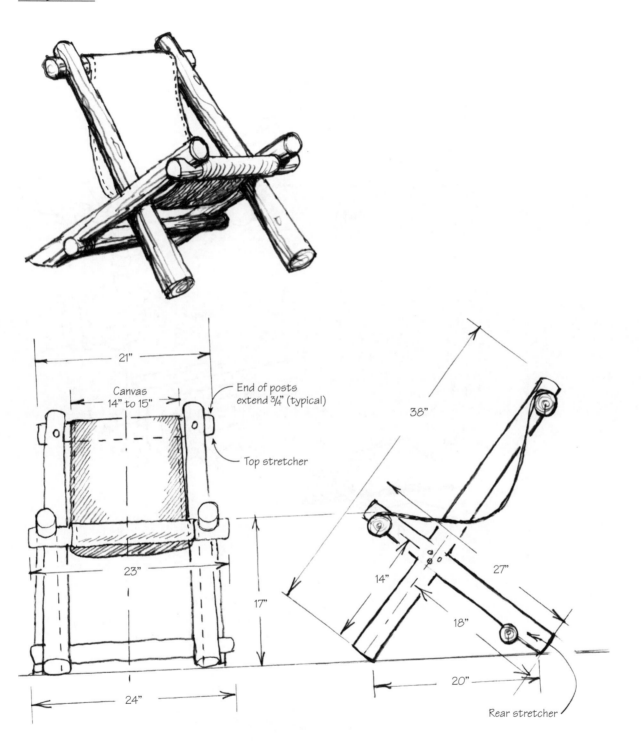

21"

Canvas
14" to 15"

End of posts
extend ¾" (typical)

Top stretcher

23"

24"

17"

38"

14"

27"

18"

20"

Rear stretcher

Cutting a "Lincoln Log" Notch

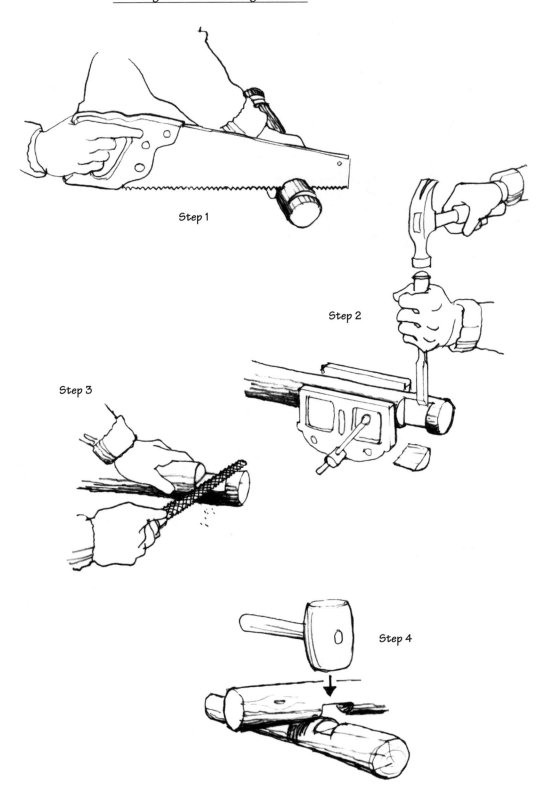

Step 1

Step 2

Step 3

Step 4

test fitting them until they line up perfectly. Note that, for stability, the top of the chair is not as wide as the bottom therefore you need to angle your joints accordingly.

Once the pieces are put together, cut a piece of heavy canvas for the sling seat. Canvas can be found at awning shops or even art supply stores. Before cutting, mark the canvas by snapping a chalkline. The finished size should be approximately 40" long, 15" wide at the top and 16 1/2" wide at the bottom. To be safe, cut the pieces a little long and adjust the size of the canvas to fit the chair. Staple the canvas to the underneath side of the front stretchers. Use only a few staples at first and test the chair by sitting in it. Remove the staples and readjust the length of the canvas to fit your body.

Chairs, Benches, Stools and Tables Made from Logs

Make your own designs or use these for inspiration, all made from logs. Curved pieces of wood are difficult, but not impossible, to find in the woods so take your time when looking. To give your furniture a professional look and to eliminate splinters, chamfer the edges with a knife and smooth with sandpaper.

A stool can be made from a log end and some branches just by boring four holes in the log end and attaching legs.

Hollow stumps can often be found in the woods. Cut the stump as close to the base as possible and screw a section of a larger tree to the stump. Cover the screwheads with wood plugs.

A bench can be made out of pieces of slab wood by joining two pieces of wood with two cleat logs, notched and screwed from underneath.

Find an unseasoned log, saw it in half and sand the top (or seat) smooth. Bore four 1 1/2" diameter leg holes at a 10-degree angle, so that the legs will be splayed out. Cut a slot in the top end of each leg and partially insert a hardwood wedge into the slot. Hammer a leg into each hole. When the wedge reaches the end of the hole, it will force itself into the slot and expand the tenon inside the hole.

Log Furniture Ideas

Log Bench

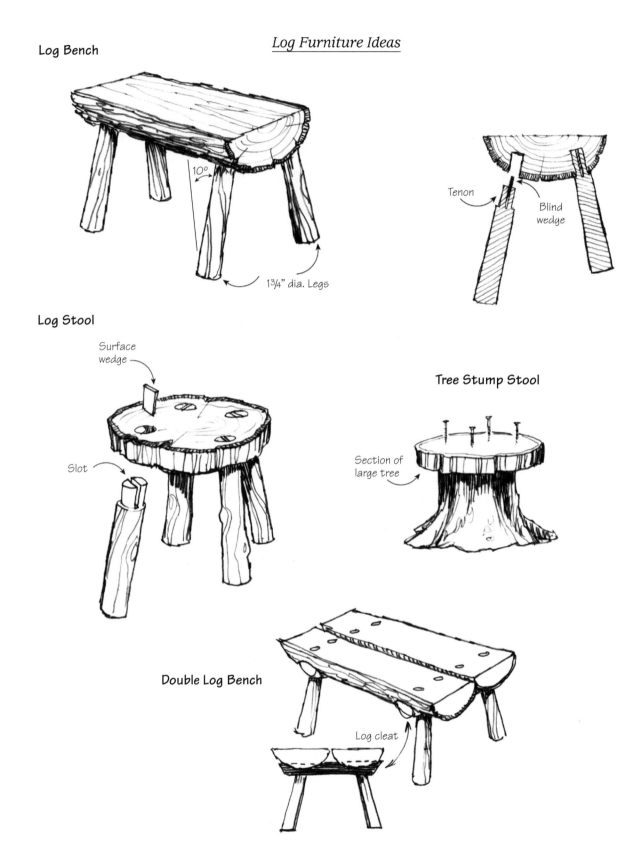

10°

1¾" dia. Legs

Tenon

Blind wedge

Log Stool

Surface wedge

Slot

Tree Stump Stool

Section of large tree

Double Log Bench

Log cleat

Log Furniture Ideas

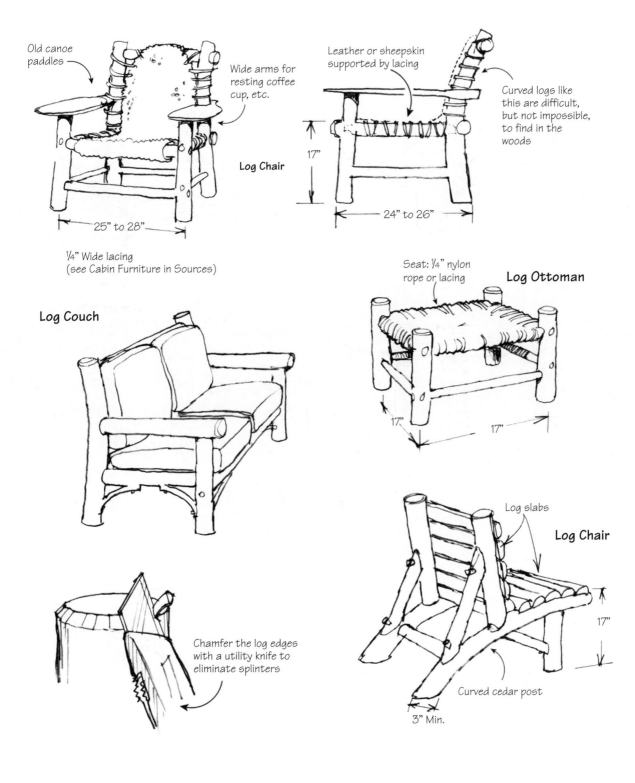

Old canoe paddles

Wide arms for resting coffee cup, etc.

Log Chair

25" to 28"

¼" Wide lacing
(see Cabin Furniture in Sources)

Leather or sheepskin supported by lacing

Curved logs like this are difficult, but not impossible, to find in the woods

17"

24" to 26"

Seat: ¼" nylon rope or lacing

Log Ottoman

17"   17"

Log Couch

Chamfer the log edges with a utility knife to eliminate splinters

Log slabs

Log Chair

17"

Curved cedar post

3" Min.

Cabin Furniture: Tables

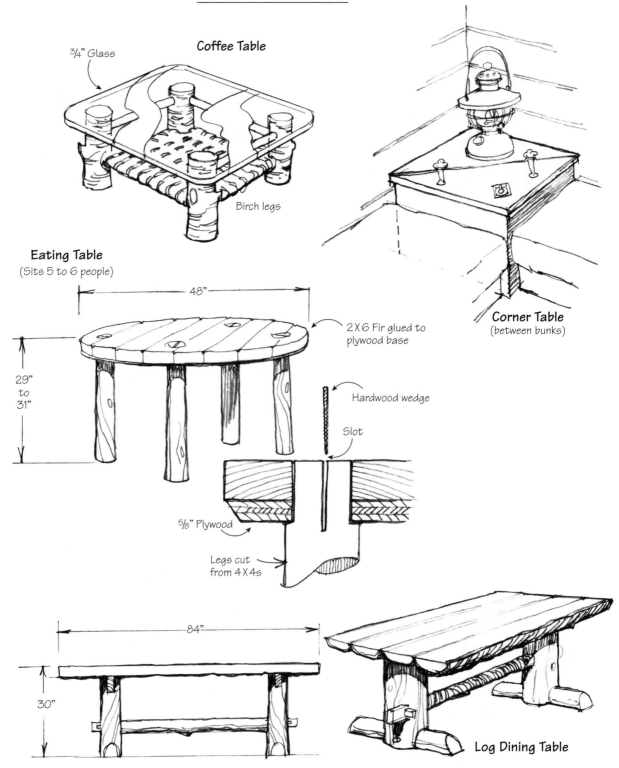

Coffee Table

¾" Glass

Birch legs

Corner Table
(between bunks)

Eating Table
(Sits 5 to 6 people)

48"

2 X 6 Fir glued to
plywood base

Hardwood wedge

Slot

29"
to
31"

⅝" Plywood

Legs cut
from 4 X 4s

84"

30"

Log Dining Table

Cabin Furniture: Tables & Benches

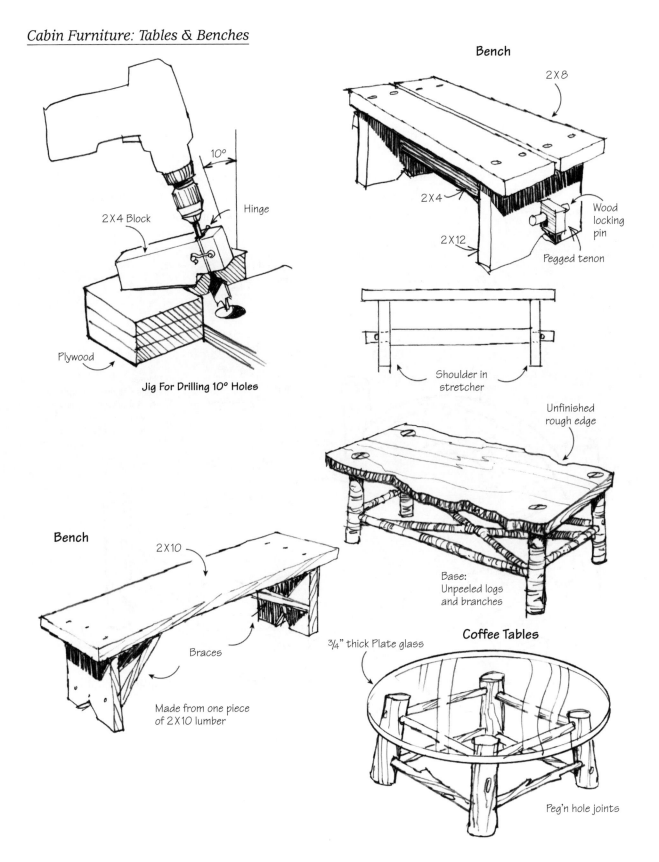

10°

2 X 4 Block

Hinge

Plywood

Jig For Drilling 10° Holes

Bench

2 X 8

2 X 4

2 X 12

Wood
locking
pin

Pegged tenon

Shoulder in
stretcher

Unfinished
rough edge

Base:
Unpeeled logs
and branches

Bench

2 X 10

Braces

Made from one piece
of 2 X 10 lumber

Coffee Tables

¾" thick Plate glass

Peg'n hole joints

Beds

Buy the mattress and boxspring first, before building your cabin beds. Otherwise, you may find that the mattress does not fit the bed you've built. The platform bed is the easiest bed to build. It is basically a box with a plywood bedboard that can be lifted up to access storage space underneath. Fold-out bunk beds are a great space saver for a small cabin bedroom. Make your own mattress using 2" soft foam, covered with a piece of cotton or canvas fabric. When not in use, the extra bed folds back to make one 4" thick bed or couch.

Bed Sizes

Type	Mattress
Twin	38" X 75"
Double	54" X 75"
Queen	60" X 80"
Bunk	30" X 75"
	33" X 75"
Camp	25" X 77"
	20" X 72"

Note:
Since sizes vary according to manufacturer always buy the mattress first before building the bed

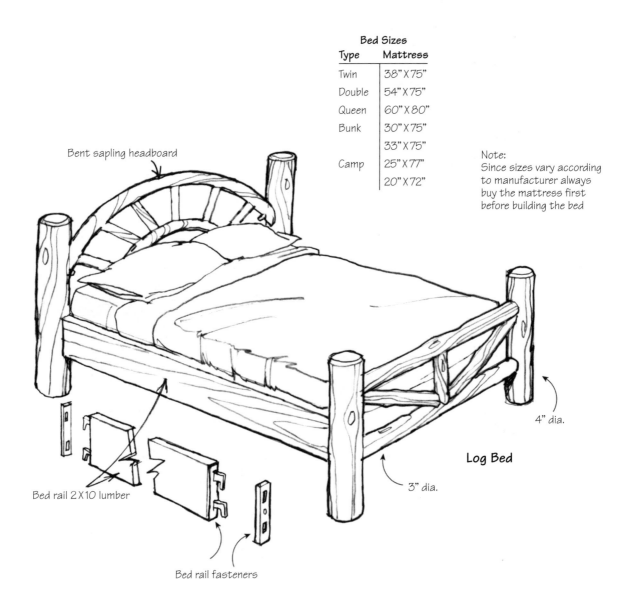

Bent sapling headboard

4" dia.

Log Bed

3" dia.

Bed rail 2 X 10 lumber

Bed rail fasteners

Cabin Furniture: Beds

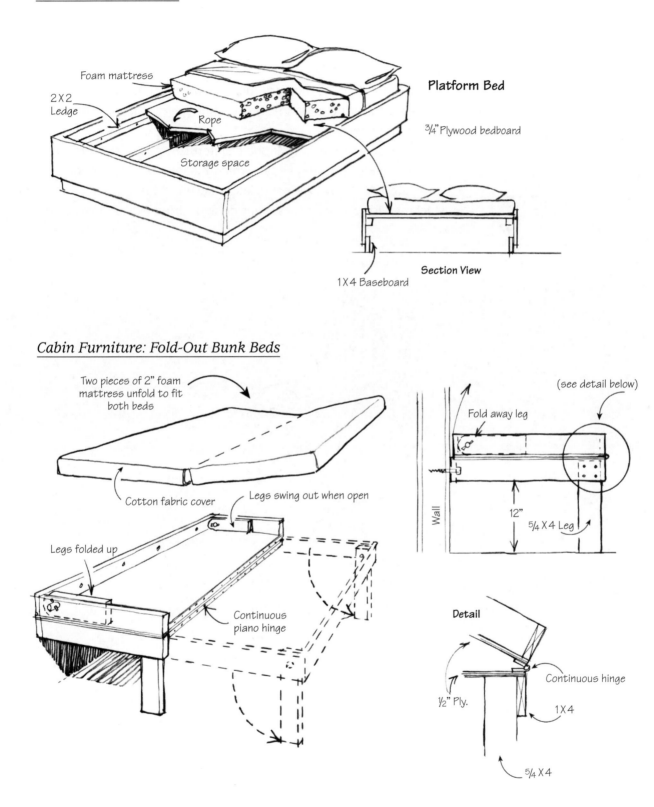

Foam mattress

2 X 2 Ledge

Rope

Storage space

Platform Bed

3/4" Plywood bedboard

Section View

1 X 4 Baseboard

Cabin Furniture: Fold-Out Bunk Beds

Two pieces of 2" foam mattress unfold to fit both beds

Cotton fabric cover

Legs swing out when open

Legs folded up

Continuous piano hinge

(see detail below)

Fold away leg

Wall

12"

5/4 X 4 Leg

Detail

Continuous hinge

1/2" Ply.

1 X 4

5/4 X 4

Chairs

For cabin dwellers who are not inclined to build their furniture, two classic styles that are well suited for most cabins are snowshoe furniture and Adirondack chairs.

Carefully made, this furniture is lightweight and durable. Most snowshoe furniture is hand-crafted from select Vermont white ash and natural rawhide.

The classic Adirondack chair epitomizes cabin style. The best ones are made from red cedar, which makes them light enough to move around easily. We especially like the "canoe paddle" arms which provide a place to rest your book or drink (see Sources).

Classic Cabin Accessories

Blankets

Outfitting your cabin with blankets is a personal decision and depends largely on how cold it gets and who will be using the cabin. If you have a cabin near the beach filled with young children and pets tracking sand and water in daily, you might consider using cotton throws as lightweight covers for cots and couches. Some of the striped Indian ones come in bright colors and can also be used as tablecloths or for beach picnics.

If, on the other hand, your cabin is deep in the north woods, or in an area that cools down at night, there is nothing warmer and more aesthetically pleasing than a thick wool blanket. Our favorite, and one of the most long-lasting woolen blankets made, is the Hudson Bay Point Blanket. Used by Admiral Byrd on his expedition to the Antarctic and by Lindbergh on his flight to Iceland, they are prized for their warmth and durability, and should last the lifetime of the cabin. Look for the "points" (short, narrow, black lines woven into the blankets) which originally represented the value of the blanket when traded with the Indians for beaver pelts (see Sources).

Cast Iron Skillet

Whether you are cooking indoors on a stove or outdoors over an open campfire, a good cast iron skillet is essential. Because cast iron distributes the heat evenly, less heat is needed to cook. Once you season a cast iron pan, a natural non-stick finish is created. If you cook outside over a campfire, another useful cast iron utensil is a Dutch oven, which hangs from a tripod and chain.

Season your cast iron pan by putting a tablespoon of vegetable shortening in the pan. Warm and coat the entire utensil with the shortening. Heat the pan upside down at 350 degrees for one hour (place foil on the oven bottom to catch any drippings). Remove from the oven and wipe with a paper towel (see Sources).

Knives

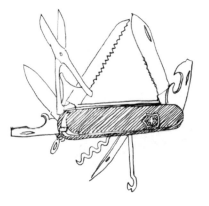

If your cabin is located in your backyard, chances are you won't need to stock it with any special tools or knives. If, however, it is in a remote area where emergencies can arise, the right knife can be essential. One of our favorites is the Swiss Army Knife. Originally made in 1891 for the Swiss Army, it quickly became the James Bond gadget of its day. It combines the pocketknife with several other tools, including a can opener, screwdriver, cork screw and hole punch. There are many variations of this knife, but a practical one for cabin living is the Rainier model, which has a saw that can cut small branches and a semi-serrated knife blade useful for everything from spreading peanut butter to scaling fish (see Sources).

Multi-Tools

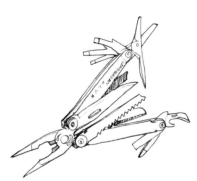

More advanced than the Swiss Army Knife, a multi-tool serves several functions in one. There are many different makes and models available, depending on your needs. We found the Leatherman Multi-Tool to work the best for us, combining a knife, file, four sizes of screwdrivers, pliers, scissors, wire cutter, saw and can opener in one pocket-sized tool. The different blades open easily and the stainless steel parts are machined to extremely high tolerance (see Sources).

A Dependable Flashlight

Whether your cabin has electric, propane or gas lighting, a good rechargeable flashlight and a stash of fully charged batteries is still essential in any cabin (even one located in your backyard!). Look for one that holds a charge longer than one weekend and has a beam that can help you find a trail even on the darkest of nights. A flashlight with a swivel head and base is useful for allowing you to stand the flashlight up when performing tasks that require two hands. DeWalt makes a 12-volt one that casts a beam almost like a car headlight when it is fully charged. It's so strong, we have even used it to spot buoys at night when we are sailing into our home port (see Sources).

Swedish Bow Saw

Since space is often limited in a cabin, it is a good idea to be selective about which tools are the most essential and deserve space. We find a good saw invaluable for a weekend cabin. We discovered the Swedish bow saw while visiting relatives in a remote part of Maine. David was asked to make a small bench for their cabin, and the only available wood was a few planks of lumber that had washed up on shore. Our hostess brought out a Swedish bow saw, and it sawed through the wood like a hot knife through butter. Besides being used for making furniture, bow saws are also used for cutting small trees and logs. We especially recommend the 21" model, with its easy-to-grip handle (see Sources).

Firebacks

A cast iron fireback, positioned against the back wall of the hearth, helps to protect the masonry of the wall and also radiates the fire's heat forward. Pennsylvania Firebacks makes several sizes and designs of firebacks, including some beautiful, historic reproductions. They come with a pair of "Saf-T-Boots," which safely support them at an angle in the back of the fireplace (see Sources).

Ecofan

For cabins heated largely by wood stoves, the Ecofan is a terrific discovery. This heat-powered fan uses no batteries or electricity and is designed to circulate the warm air created by a wood stove. The fan sits on the top of a wood-burning stove, and as the stove gets hotter, the fan runs faster. It is extremely practical for a small cabin since it measures only 8 3/4" high by 6 3/4" wide by 5 3/4" deep (see Sources).

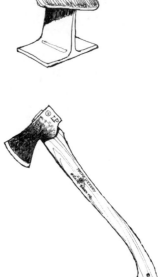

A Good Ax

For 25 years, we heated our cabin solely with firewood, therefore it was essential that we own a good ax for cutting logs. After trying out several, our favorite one was a Swedish ax made by Gränsfors Bruks, Inc. Each one is hand forged and the ax head is initialed by a master blacksmith. They are extremely sharp and come with a protective leather sheath for the head. Almost as valuable as the ax itself is the handbook that comes with each one. It contains quite useful tips on using an ax that even professional wood choppers can benefit from reading (see Sources).

Lamps and Lanterns

Every cabin needs a proper lantern whether it be for reading, eating or simply moving about at night. Having researched most of the lanterns available on the market, we have compiled the following list to help you determine what type of lantern best suits your needs (see Sources).

CANDLE LANTERNS

Long Burning Candle   Northern Lights   UCO Chandelier   UCO Mini Lantern

Pros

- 6" long candles can burn up to 14 hours.
- Dripless candles leave no mess.
- Enclosed flame won't blow out.
- Flame is brighter than kerosene lanterns.
- Lanterns are inexpensive.
- Suitable for indoor use.

Cons

- Three to six candles are necessary to read by.
- Fire hazard if not monitored properly.

KEROSENE LANTERNS

Pros

- Fuel sold in hardware stores and gas stations.
- Fuel is inexpensive.
- Long burn time between fillings.
- Lanterns are relatively inexpensive.

Cons

- Smells of kerosene oil.
- Not recommended for indoor use.
- Emits black smoke.
- Globe requires daily cleaning.
- Difficult to read by.

Dietz Kerosene Lantern

OIL LAMPS WITH FLAT WICKS

Pros

- Lamp oil does not have an unpleasant smell.
- Burns clean—can be used indoors.
- Cost-efficient.
- Safe (fuel is not under pressure).
- Lamps are inexpensive.

Cons

- Not bright enough to read by.

Oil Lamp

ALADDIN OIL LAMPS

Pros

- Give off as much light as a 60 watt bulb (six times more than kerosene lanterns).
- Large fuel capacity (24 ozs.).
- Fuel efficient —One gallon lasts 40 hours.

Cons

- Very expensive.

Aladdin Oil Lamp

PROPANE GAS LAMPS

Pros

- High output—same power as a 70 watt bulb.
- Very low maintenance.
- Burns odor and smoke free.

Cons

- Lamps are mounted on the wall or the ceiling.
- Installation requires a gas installer.

Propane Gas Wall Light

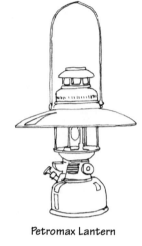

Petromax Lantern

BRIGHT WHITE LIGHT PRESSURIZED LANTERNS

Pros	Cons

Pros

- Give off as much light as three or four 100 watt bulbs.
- Burn kerosene, white gas, or Coleman fuel.
- Fuel is one-third the cost of propane.
- Requires only one filling every 5 1/2 hours of use.

Cons

- Requires hand pumping to pressurize tank.
- Makes a constant *shhh* sound.
- Recommended for outdoor use only.
- Mantles are very fragile and break easily.
- Can be scary and difficult to light.
- Very hot while burning.

RECHARGEABLE BATTERY-OPERATED LANTERN

Battery Lantern LSI Lighthawk

Pros

- Provides light at full strength for 5 hours and can be recharged in car cigarette lighter.
- Power cell lasts 10 years and can be recharged 1000 times.
- Bright Halogen lamp is easy to read by.

Cons

- Needs outside power source to recharge.

Cooking Gear

When we started building our cabin, we often used a small cast iron hibachi to grill chicken, beef or seafood kebabs. They are easy to heat up, using charcoal briquettes, and require little space for storage. Some people prefer a gas barbecue and briquettes. Today, we do most of our cooking on a simple grill placed over an outdoor campfire, made from oak wood. Jeanie's brother showed us how to increase the draft to the

fire by providing an opening at each end. We stack loose bricks on top of each other to form two crescent-shaped walls and lay the grill on top. Since the bricks are loose, they can be adjusted in height to allow for the intensity of heat required for whatever you are cooking.

Coleman sells a combination grill and burner. Although it is inexpensive, it is one of the few gas grills that burns hot enough to get food brown and sizzling. At 10,000 BTUs, the grill has temperature variations, so it cooks hotter in the center and makes adjusting your cooking temperature easier. The burner section is great for heating water, cereal, soup and sauces, and the grill side is perfect for grilling fish or steaks. The stove has an automatic (matchless) lighting system and uses propane gas.

To keep foods cool, the best non-electric cooler we have found is the Coleman "Xtreme Cooler," which will keep ice frozen for five days in hot weather. Later on, to upgrade your refrigeration, you can purchase one of the several types of mini refrigerators that run on propane gas. A mini-fridge can be installed under the counter or on top of the counter and store up to 7 cubic feet of food supplies.

First-Aid Kits

A first-aid kit is a necessary part of every cabin, especially during construction. You can buy pre-packaged first-aid kits from most camping supply stores or catalogs, but you may be paying for items that you will never use. In addition, some of the items you are most likely to need, like sunburn lotion and poison ivy cream, will probably not be included. What you should stock depends on your climate, the terrain surrounding your cabin, how far your cabin is from a hospital, and what type of injuries or emergencies you might expect.

The following is a partial list of items you might include in your first-aid kit:

1. Hydrogen peroxide to sterilize cuts.

2. Bacitracin to prevent infection in minor cuts.

3. Ibuprofen tablets for aching backs and muscles.

4. Hydrocortisone ointment for insect bites.

5. Antihistamine (e.g., Contact) for bee stings.

6. Sunscreen to prevent sunburn and a medicated first-aid spray (like Solarcaine) to use in case you forgot to put on the sunscreen.

7. Poison ivy lotion (before and after types).

8. Band-Aids, gauze and adhesive tape.

9. Butterfly closure strips for closing open wounds.

10. Tweezers for removing splinters.

11. Snakebite kit.

Protecting Your Cabin

Fire Prevention

Nothing could be sadder than to arrive at your cabin and find only smoldering remains. Fire prevention is important and should be taken seriously. Every room in a cabin should have a handy, working fire extinguisher and a smoke alarm. When planning and building your cabin, give some thought as to how you and any other occupants will exit in the event of a fire. Once your cabin is built, periodically practice fire drills and discuss appropriate evacuation procedures.

Fires are most likely to occur around your chimney, cooking stove or in front of your fireplace where sparks might jump out and ignite a rug or something else flammable. It is a good idea to keep a bucket of water ready to throw on the fire in case of an emergency. In our cabin we keep a plastic 5 gallon pail of water next to the fireplace. To prevent it from freezing when the cabin is not in use, we put a little antifreeze in with the water with a warning on the outside "Warning—poison—water not safe for drinking."

For grease fires, 5 lb. boxes of baking soda should be kept near the stove, as well as a chemical fire extinguisher. Look for the initials ABC on the side of the extinguisher, which means that it serves both grease and paper fires. If you do have a fire, aim the nozzle at the source of the fire, not the smoke. Make a point of checking the gauges every year to make sure they are "in the green" and fully charged.

If your cabin has water under pressure, keep a hose hooked up outside even in the winter to handle fires on the roof or inside. If your cabin does not have running water, invest in a hand pump with a portable tank that can be carried to the source of the fire.

Check with your local fire company to find out what they require in the way of access roads. Make sure that your access road is wide enough for a fire truck to reach your cabin and that there is a place for it to turn around. We know of a house that burned to the ground because the driveway was too steep for the fire trucks.

Cabin Security

A good idea put to use by friends of ours who live in a difficult to reach camp in Maine is an air horn that can be used to summon help. The sound travels across the water and, hopefully, help arrives quickly by boat.

To lock or not to lock the door is a question facing every cabin owner. If you don't leave anything in your cabin worth stealing and you don't mind people staying there, you might consider leaving your cabin unlocked, hoping others will treat it with respect, leaving it as they found it. Some cabins, such as Adirondack lean-tos, are always left open and used by campers and hikers on an honor system of leaving enough firewood for the next visitor to start a campfire. Some huts, situated along the Appalachian Trail near Franconia Notch, are not only stocked with firewood, but with food as well. One law of the wilderness, according to the legendary outdoorsman D.C. Beard, is that even horse thieves and bandits respect a cabin left unattended. However, if you prefer to protect your cabin from people who may be in the area, there are several things you can do.

The first line of defense, and the easiest to install, are signs posted on trees, letting intruders know they are trespassing on private property. Post signs in several places along any public road bordering your property so there is no excuse for trespassers not to see them.

To make sure the signs aren't removed, hang them at least 9' or 10' up on a tree.

The second line of defense should be installing a gate at the beginning of any trail or driveway that accesses your property, making it more difficult for uninvited guests to reach your cabin. We built a 12' wide swinging gate out of pressure-treated 1x6 lumber and hung it from heavy-duty galvanized gate hinges at one end, and a hasp and padlock at the other end. We installed a second gate further up the road, and hooked it up to a battery operated alarm that activated when the gate was lifted off the post. A small sign reads "Warning—this gate is electronically controlled and will sound an alarm if moved." People can always find a way around or over gates; however, both signs and gates are deterrents that send a clear message to trespassers to think twice before they invade private property.

Strong doors and windows are another way you can protect your cabin from uninvited guests or intruders. Doors should be a minimum of 1 1/2" thick and partially made of plywood. Install your door to swing out, not in, so that it can't be kicked in, since it will be resting against the door frame. Instead of installing a door handle, which can help an intruder pull open a door, use the key as your handle. Hide the key on a nail, attached to a tree, some distance away in the woods.

The lightweight door jambs that the hinges are attached to should be screwed securely to the heavier framing inside the cabin wall, using extra long screws to prevent intruders from prying the jambs away from the door. Use a minimum of three 3 1/2" long, galvanized butt hinges. Replace the screws that come with the hinges with 2 1/2" screws that go all the way into the wall.

To prevent broken windows, instead of using glass, make your window panes out of 1/8" thick clear Lexan, a strong unbreakable plastic. Make strong frames for the Lexan window panes, using 2x3 lumber, held shut by two slide bolts on the inside.

Another way to protect your cabin when you are not there, and to give you privacy when you are home, is to install strong shutters on the outside of the windows. To close up the shutters when you are leaving, remove the screen and place a short 2x4 across both shutters held in place by two "L" brackets sold in most lumber yards.

The most serious threat to our cabin was vandalism by kids who considered it a challenge to see if they could get inside. Chances are, if someone is breaking into your cabin (especially kids), they will make a lot of noise. Talk with your neighbors and tell them to feel free to question strangers who they see walking on your land or acting suspiciously noisy and to ask them to identify themselves.

Cabin Security

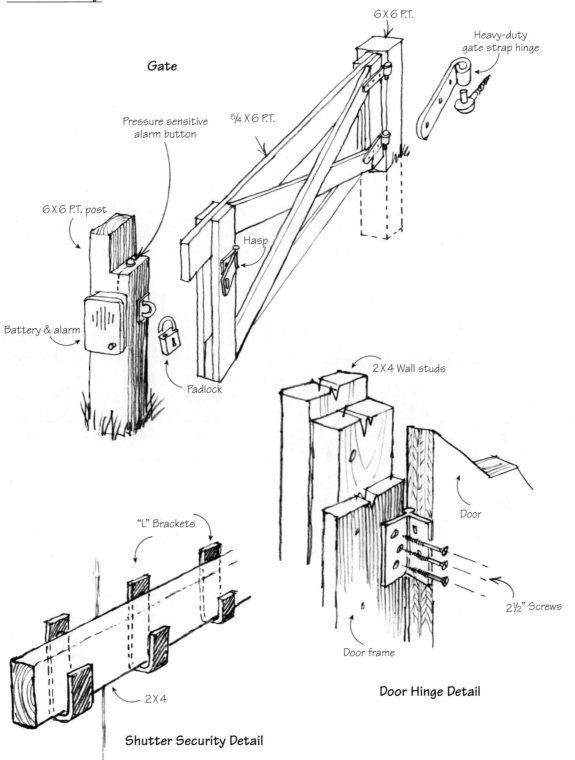

6 X 6 P.T.

Heavy-duty
gate strap hinge

Gate

Pressure sensitive
alarm button

5/4 X 6 P.T.

6 X 6 P.T. post

Hasp

Battery & alarm

Padlock

2 X 4 Wall studs

Door

Door frame

2½" Screws

Door Hinge Detail

"L" Brackets

2 X 4

Shutter Security Detail

One way to be forewarned if a visitor or an intruder is approaching by car is to install a motion detector alarm at the beginning of your access road. This simple device consists of a 5"x5" transmitter, with a range of 500'. The detector is wired to your cabin and buried underground near your driveway. It detects any metal vehicle that drives past the sensor, alerting you by sounding a signal and giving you time to look out the window.

To detect people walking on foot, there is another type of battery operated transmitter that can be mounted on a tree or post, located on the side of your access road. It transmits an invisible beam from as far away as 80' and is programmed so that the beam will not detect animals under 3' tall (like raccoons and skunks). It will, however, detect an occasional deer. Both transmitters send a radio signal back to the cabin where an electronic receiver sets off an alarm or whistle.

Pests

Once you have fortified your cabin against two-legged uninvited intruders, you can concentrate on the four-legged variety. Years ago, we had a real problem with raccoons. One evening, we opened up our trash shed to see four pair of eyes starring up at us. As cute as they are, raccoons are often a nuisance, spreading garbage all over the yard as they search for the perfect morsel.

Our solution was to take a garden hose (one with a pistol-shaped nozzle on the end) and wire it to the garbage can so that when the raccoon lifts up the lid of the can, the hose automatically goes on, spraying the raccoon with a blast of cold water. You will need to experiment a little to get this to work just right, but the results are worth it.

Discouraging Raccoons

Wire

BIBLIOGRAPHY

Alexander, Christopher. *A Pattern Language: Towns, Buildings, Construction*. 1977, Oxford University Press.

Berg, Donald. *Barns and Backbuildings*. 1998, Edited by Donald J. Berg, AIA.

Birch, Monte. *Complete Guide to Building Log Homes*. 1990, Sterling Publishing Co.

Burns, Max. *Cottage Water Systems: An Out-of-the City Guide to Pumps, Plumbing, Water Purification, and Privies*. 1993, Cottage Life Books.

Busha, William. *The Book of Heat*. 1982, The Stephen Green Press.

Hunt, W. Ben. *How to Build and Furnish a Log Cabin: The Easy Natural Way Using Only Hand Tools and the Woods Around You*. 1996, IDG Books.

Kylloe, Ralph. *Rustic Style*. 1998, Harry N. Abrams.

Mack, Daniel. *Making Rustic Furniture*. 1996, Lark Books.

Mason, Bernard S. *Woodcraft and Camping*. 1974, Dover Publications.

McRaven, Charles. *Building and Restoring the Hewn Log House*. 1994, Betterway Publications.

Rustrum, Calvin. *The Wilderness Cabin*. 1961, Collier Books.

Schwenke, Karl, and Sue Schwenke. *Build Your Own Stone House: Using the Easy Slipform Method*. 1991, Storey Books.

Seddon, Leigh. *Practical Pole Building Construction: With Plans for Barns, Cabins, and Outbuildings*. 1985, Williamson Pub.

Stiles, David. *Sheds: The Do-It-Yourself Guide for Backyard Builders*, Revised and Expanded. 1997, Firefly Books.

Stiles, David and Jeanie. *Garden Retreats: A Build-It-Yourself Guide*. 1999, Storey Books.

Stiles, David and Jeanie. *Playhouses You Can Build, Indoor and Backyard Design*. 1998, Firefly Books.

Stiles, David and Jeanie. *Rustic Retreats: A Build-It-Yourself Guide*. 1998, Storey Books.

Stiles, David and Jeanie. *Tree Houses You Can Actually Build*. 1998, Houghton Mifflin.

SOURCES

Tools and Hardware

BAILEY'S
P.O. Box 550
44650 Hwy. 101
Laytonville, CA 95454
800-322-4539
www.baileys-online.com
(Logging tools, log cabin building tools, portable saw mills, chain saws, axes)

DEFENDER MARINE SUPPLY
42 Great Neck Rd.
Waterford, CT 06385
800-628-8225
www.DefenderUS.com
(Extensive source of marine equipment that can be adapted to cabins, i.e., nautical hardware, cookstoves, lamps, hatches, louvers & teak products)

DEWALT INDUSTRIAL TOOL CO.
P.O. Box 158
626 Hanover Pike
Hampstead, MD
800-433-9258
www.dewalt.com

DULUTH TRADING CO.
2218 Fourth Ave. W.
Williston, ND 58801
800-505-8888
www.duluthtrading.com
(Canvas tool buckets, bags and boxes)

GEMPLER'S
100 Countryside Dr.
P.O. Box 270
Belleville, WI 53508
800-382-8473
www.gemplers.com
(Farming tools, cart wheels and tires, first-aid kits)

HARBOR FREIGHT TOOLS
3491 Mission Oaks Blvd.
Camarillo, CA 93011-6010
800-423-2567
www.harborfreight.com
(Good prices for power tools and hand woodworking tools, wood and gas stoves, generators, chain saws, water pumps, jacks and lamps. Free shipping.)

LEHMAN'S HARDWARE & APPLIANCES, INC.
Non-Electric Catalog
One Lehman Circle
P.O. Box 41
Kidron, OH 44636
888-438-5346
www.Lehmans.com
(Extensive list of useful items for outfitting cabins, i.e., wood-burning stoves, lanterns & candles, gas operated refrigerators, composting toilets, hand operated water pumps, log building tools and farm equipment)

A.M. LEONARD
241 Fox Dr.
P.O. Box 816
Piqua, OH 45356
800-543-8955
www.amleo.com
(Tree maintenance equipment, shovels & land clearing tools)

NORTHERN PROFESSIONAL EQUIPMENT & SUPPLY
P.O. Box 1499
Burnsville, MN 55337-0499
(Wagon wheels & industrial equipment including generators and hitches)

WOODWORKER'S SUPPLY
1108 North Glenn Rd.
Casper, WY 82601
800-645-9292
(Woodworking hand tools)

Camping Equipment

BEAVER TREE KITCHEN
P.O. Box 97
Fall Creek, WI 54742
www.beavertree.com
(Camp kitchen)

THE BOUNDARY WATERS
Piragis Northwoods Co.
105 North Central Ave.
Ely, MN 55731
800-223-6565
www.piragis.com
(Canoes & accessories, snowshoes, outdoor clothing, wilderness books)

CABELA'S
One Cabela Dr.
Sidney, NE 69160-9555
800-237-4444
www.cabelas.com
(Lanterns & flashlights, outdoor cooking equipment, binoculars)

CAMPMOR
P.O. Box 700
Saddle River, NJ 07458-0700
800-226-7667
www.campmor.com
(Portable showers & toilets, tents, blankets, sleeping bags, cookware & flashlights)

THE COLEMAN CO., INC.
P.O. Box 2931
Wichita, KS 67201
800-835-3278
www.coleman.com
(Mattresses & sleeping bags, lanterns & flashlights, cooking stoves & grills, generators, portable showers, water jugs & coolers)

E-Z CAMPING
P.O. Box 831343
San Antonio, TX 78283
800-535-6291
(Portable camp stoves & grills, chuck boxes)

REI
1700 45th St. E.
Sumner, WA 98390
800-426-4840
www.rei.com
(Outdoor clothing and some camping equipment)

Cabin Furniture

COUNTRY WAYS
6001 Lyndale Ave. S., Suite A
Minneapolis, MN 55419
800-216-0710
www.snowshoe.com
(Snowshoe furniture and kits for making your
own, including snowshoe lacing)

A.M. LEONARD
(see Tools and Hardware)
(Adirondack chairs, carts)

VERMONT SNOWSHOE FURNITURE
179 Mill St.
P.O. Box 312
East Barre, VT 05649
802-476-4303
www.vtsnowshoefurniture.com
(Snowshoe furniture, firewood racks)

Logs and Log Building

AUTHENTIC LOG HOMES
P.O. Box 1288
Laramie, WY 82070
307-742-3786
(Log cabin logs)

BAILEY'S
(see Tools and Hardware)

SASHCO "LOG JAM," "LOG BUILDER"
10300 E. 107th Pl.
Brighton, CO 80601
800-767-5656
www.sashco.com
(Chinking)

Lighting

(Also see Camping Equipment)

ALADDIN INDUSTRIES, LLC
ALADDIN MANTLE LAMP CO.
1741 Elm Hill Pike
Nashville, TN 37210
800-457-5267
www.aladdinlamps.com
(Lamps)

LSI
6410 West Ridge Rd.
Erie, PA 16506-1023
800-631-3814
www.flashlight.com
(Night Hawk rechargeable lantern)

NORTHERN LIGHTS
P.O. Box 2692
Truckee, CA 96160
530-550-0738
www.candlelanterns.com
(Candle lanterns)

PAULIN HUMPHREY
B.P. Products
4780 Beidler Rd.
Willoughby, OH 44094
800-760-1957
www.bpproducts.com
(Gas lights)

D.L. SCHWARTZ CO.
2188 S. US HWY 27
Berne, IN 46711
219-692-6818
(Dietz lanterns)

UCO CORP.
9225 151st Ave. NE
Redmond, WA 98052
425-883-6600
www.ucocorp.com
(Three candle lanterns)

Utilities and Appliances

ACME KITCHEN CORP.
P.O. Box 348
Hudson, NY 12534
518-828-4191
www.acmekitchenettes.com
(Mini 3-in-1 kitchen)

COLEMAN POWERMATE INC.
4970 Airport Rd.
Kearney, NE 68848
800-445-1805
www.colemanpowermate.com
(Generators)

DEEP ROCK
2209 Anderson Rd.
Opelika, AL 36803
800-333-7762
www.deeprock.com
(Well drilling equipment)

VORNADO AIR CIRCULATION SYSTEMS, INC.
415 East 13th St.
Andover, KS 67002
800-297-0883
www.vornado.com
(Electric heaters)

SELKIRK METALBESTOS
An Eljer Industries Co.
P.O. Box 372
Nampa, ID 83653-0372
(Stove pipe chimney)

Sanitary Systems

INCINOLET
2639 Andjon
Dallas, TX 75220
800-527-5551
www.incinolet.com
(Electric toilet)

RELIANCE PRODUCTS L.P.
1093 Sherwin Rd.
Winnipeg, Man. Canada R3H 1A4
800-665-0258
(Luggable loo and water jugs)

SUN-MAR
600 Main St.
Tonawanda, NY 14150-0888
1-800-461-2461
www.sun-mar.com
(Composting toilet)

Cabin Kits

SHELTER-KIT INC.
22 Mill St.
P.O. Box 1
Tilton, NH 03276
603-286-7611
www.shelter-kit.com

SHELTER INSTITUTE
38 Center St.
Bath, ME 04530
207-442-7938
www.shelterinstitute.com

Classic Cabin Accessories

HUDSON BAY POINT BLANKET
Woolrich, Inc.
Woolrich, PA 17779
800-995-1299
www.woolrich.com

SWEDISH BOW SAW
BAHCO (Sandvik) Tools
P.O. Box 2036
Scranton, PA 18501
717-341-9500

CAST IRON SKILLET
Lodge Manufacturing Co.
P.O. Box 380
6th St.
South Pittsburgh TN 37380
423-837-7181
www.lodgemfg.com

ECOFAN
Caframo Ltd.
R.R. 2
Wiarton, ON
Canada N0H 2T0
800-567-3556
www.caframo.com

LEATHERMAN "WAVE" MULTI-TOOL
Leatherman Tool Group Inc.

12106 N.E. Ainsworth Circle
Portland, OR 97220
503-253-7826
www.leatherman.com

FIREBACK
Pennsylvania Firebacks Inc.
2237 Bethel Rd.
Lansdale, PA 19446
888-349-3002
www.fireback.com

SWISS ARMY KNIVES
Swiss Army Brands, Inc.
One Research Dr.
P.O. Box 874
Shelton, CN 06484-0874
800-442-2706
www.swissarmy.com

Wenger
15 Corp Dr.
Orangeburg, NY 10962
800-431-2996
www.wengerna.com

SWEDISH AX
Gränsfors Bruks, Inc.
821 West 5th North St.
P.O. Box 818
Summerville, SC 29484
800-433-2863
www.gransfors.com

RECHARGEABLE FLASHLIGHT
DeWalt Industrial Tool Co.
P.O. Box 158
626 Hanover Pike
Hampstead, MD
800-433-9258

INDEX

NOTES

NOTES

NOTES

NOTES

NOTES

NOTES

NOTES

Note to Readers:

Since many of our readers invariably change our plans to fit their particular needs, we have purposely omitted exact specifications and dimensions. We assume that the reader will seek qualified, licensed architects or engineers to make more detailed plans for submission to their local building and health departments, as required.

If you have built your own cabin, we would be most interested
in seeing a photo of your project. Please send it to:
David & Jeanie Stiles
161 East 91 St.
New York, NY
10128
U.S.A.

You can write to us at jeandave@aol.com
or visit our website at www.stilesdesigns.com